W9-DHW-327

Library of Congress Cataloging-in-Publication Data
Simply Brilliant / by Thomas J. Leonard
p. cm.
ISBN 1-929668-00-7

Copy editing by Randa McIntosh
Layout and Design by Cosmyk Images, Miami, Florida.

Printed in the United States of America
10 9 8 7 6 5 4 3 2 1

Published by Coach U Press
PO Box 881595
Steamboat Springs, Colorado 80488

SIMPLY BRILLIANT

1800 SUCCESS TIPS AND LIFE LESSONS
FROM AMERICA'S TOP PERSONAL AND BUSINESS COACHES

THOMAS J. LEONARD
COACH U PRESS

"The only things worth learning are the things you learn after you know it all." - *Harry Truman*

INTRODUCTION

What is wisdom today?
Is wisdom a set of principles or laws?
Does wisdom come to the lucky individual with
good genes and smart memes?
Does wisdom come from a group with special
access to "the truth?"
Or, is wisdom something that is alive, constantly
developing and evolving as we humans evolve?

Perhaps we'll never know. In fact, to study wisdom is
perhaps to restrict it. I think I'd rather just benefit from
wisdom, whatever its source. What you'll be enjoying in
these pages is the collective wisdom (I suppose that term is
redundant – I mean, how can wisdom be anything other
than collective?) of dozens of personal and professional
coaches who trained at Coach U. These coaches have come
from virtually all personal and professional backgrounds:
business consultants, therapists, attorneys, physicians,
ministers, writers, educators and more. You name it and
they've been there. What they bring with them is what
they've learned in their own experience – and what they've
learned from clients. In fact, coaches have coached over
1,000,000 individuals worldwide since the profession got its
start in 1988 when I began training the first 12 coaches
via Coach U.

One of these first coaches was Sandy Vilas, who is now the
owner and CEO of Coach U, the worldwide leader in
coach training. I am grateful to the coaches who
generously shared their wisdom with us in these pages.

Thomas J. Leonard
April 26, 1999

Dedicated to the thousands of Coach U-trained coaches who willingly share their wisdom every day.

I Have Learned...

... that my present is perfect.

... that any two people are not well-matched unless they have comparable amounts of courage plus a well-matched desire for change.

... that my body can sense the incongruity of someone's actions not reflecting their words.

... that we find God through truth.

... that coaches do not fix problems; they support people who are ready to own their lives.

... that no life accomplishment is worth anything in the absence of relationships.

... that the voices that whisper messages of doubt are outside our minds, apart from who we truly are.

... that the mirror doesn't lie.

... that if you put enough of the right structures in place, you will move forward more effortlessly.

... that great coaches can articulate in twenty-five words or less their coaching gifts.

... that the heaviest thing in the world may not be an element after all, but an attitude – apathy.

... not to lend or invest any more money than I can afford to lose.

... to enjoy life's moments and to release them lovingly as they pass.

... to turn off the radio while I drive to allow my mind to bask in the silence.

I have learned that the mirror

does not lie.

I Have Learned...

... that believing in a friendly Universe is a good
place to start.

... that dogs will reveal everything there is to know about
being joyfully present if we just pay attention.

... that an efficient solution to a problem may not be the
most effective.

... that communicating my unhappiness is not the same as
communicating what I want or need.

... that adults have a "story," an agenda, and an evil twin.
To have a successful relationship, you have to get
through the story, then negotiate an agenda that's
acceptable to the evil twin.

... that added value is always the best sales tool.

... that if I think they're diamonds, they're diamonds.

... that projects have to be sold three times — first at the
original sale, then at project's start-up, and finally at
completion.

... that my most important mission is to be kind to
myself and others.

... that being alone often provides a sense of great fullness.

... that when I feel disappointed in someone, it's usually
due to my expectations rather than their actions.

... that when a situation seems immovable, drastic action in
any direction will create the desired results.

... that maximum profitability exists at the brink of disaster.

... that it is more important to be consistent than it is
to be exact.

... to use pencil to write in my daily planner.

... that relationships are like the weather – sunny people provide warmth, stormy people provide rain.

... that information is of no use if I can't remember where I jotted it down.

... that if someone in America and in China point "up" simultaneously, they end up pointing in opposite directions.

... that if I'm stuck, to invent a ridiculous solution then sleep on it.

... that when dealing with professionals, if I'm not clear about what I want, I'll wind up with what they want.

... that it saves time to always put my watch, keys, and wallet in the same place every day.

... that the more we chase a career, the more it eludes us.

... that small mistakes prevent big failures.

... that any step toward a goal is a step in the right direction, even if some of them are missteps.

... that when we water the seeds of our interest, they grow.

... that life doesn't wait.

... that effortless selling depends upon a well-articulated USP (unique selling proposition).

... that control, like magic, is just an illusion.

... that a relationship without commitment is just an acquaintance.

I Have Learned...

... that all emotional pain stems from resistance and a sense of what "should" be.

... that traveling at high speed through the fog of change will lead to a crash.

... that even if I choose not to decide I have still made a choice.

... that although people say they feel better after indulging in something addictive, what they actually feel is numb.

... that both loving and hating involve a lot of energy; the former gives it whereas the latter drains it.

... that true leaders listen more than they speak.

... that dogs hold the secret to being happy and loving, but I haven't learned how they do it yet.

... that blame evokes defensiveness and that defensiveness reduces awareness.

... that true leaders makes decisions by using their hearts as well as their minds.

... that true leaders understand ancient truths and laws of human nature.

... that the Creator gave us creativity and we invented control.

... that if there's drama in the air, someone is about to become "shark-bait."

... that a dream is like a sculpture that must be chipped away until it's complete.

... that not only is control impossible to maintain, but trying to keep it consumes energy.

I have learned that
dogs will reveal everything there is to
know about being joyfully present
if we just pay attention.

I Have Learned...

... that counting to ten is actually brilliant.

... that worms believe the whole world is dirty, and that people sometimes think a lot like worms.

... that the extent to which I forgive myself for my mistakes, misjudgments and screw-ups is the extent to which I can become fully present.

... that people are far more noble than any of their belief systems.

... that it is only by embracing my "shadow" that can I truly begin to love myself.

... that good fortune almost always shows up in the form of another person.

... that when I'm hurting too much to cry, laughter is the only sensible response.

... that since there's no surviving this lifetime, I may as well take every risk that will let me make the most of this experience.

... that life is a game, a fact we tend to lose sight of when we think we're losing.

... that my need to look good has ended up screwing me up more than just about anything else.

... that all the events, circumstances, and people in my life were there to prepare me for this moment.

... that life is like a double-blind experiment; we don't know where we came from or where we're going, so what really matters is what we do right now.

... that alternatives are more effective than ultimatums.

BUSINESS REPLY MAIL
FIRST-CLASS MAIL   PERMIT NO. 8456   DES MOINES IA

POSTAGE WILL BE PAID BY ADDRESSEE

FamilyFun

PO BOX 37033
BOONE IA 50037-2033

A Special Invitation...

FamilyFun

invites you to sit back and save ... enjoying free home-delivery
of each issue at 62% off the cover price!

10 issues (1 year) just $14.95.

J5PS2

Name
_____
please print

Address _____ Apt. _____

City _____ State _____ Zip _____

E-mail Address*
_____

*By providing my e-mail address, I am indicating I'd like to receive information
about my subscription and special offers from FamilyFun via e-mail.

☐ Payment Enclosed   ☐ Bill Me Later

... that an attitude of gratitude is a great source for abundance.

... that making a difference is what life is all about.

... if I ever want to know how a person conducts business to suggest a day of golf.

... that discounting another is one way I try to disown the unacceptable aspects of my Self.

... that people tend to meditate when their lives feel like they're falling apart. Then, when things get better, they stop.

... that transformation lives in action.

... that it's ok not to know the exact right word for something – describing it is often more fun.

... that real power comes from my ability to focus.

... that courage only shows up in the presence, not in the absence, of fear.

... that often the most destructive ideas are not the ones I think, but the ones that think me.

... that only as I love and respect others will I be able to love and respect myself.

... that God can only work through those whose feet are planted firmly on the ground.

... that the more we learn about receiving gracefully, the more skillful we become at giving joyfully.

... that to fully heal, one must release the memory of pain from body, mind and spirit.

I Have Learned...

... that good food makes people happy.

... that courage is not the absence of fear but the mastery of it.

... that getting permission from self is more important than getting it from others.

... that until we look at our shadow side and understand it, it will lurk and haunt us forever.

... that our friends don't want us to have all the answers.

... that we are truly alone, but that it is best spelled "all one."

... that having a role model is one of the smartest and smoothest ways to succeed.

... that I am calmer and more effective when I am well rested.

... that growing often means letting go of former beliefs.

... that when I hear with my heart, body and soul, I am able to reflect the truth that a person is ready to hear.

... that developing reserves creates more freedom in my life.

... that until we actually live in our bodies, feel our hearts and understand our pain we have not fully lived.

... that generosity without strong boundaries results in being taken from instead of received from.

... that miraculous solutions appear out of nowhere once we become open and aware.

... that life is easier when my handbag is organized.

... that thriving relationships with others require fully understanding my relationship with Self.

I have learned that

promises are sacred.

I Have Learned...

... that money is a means to an end and that end is not necessarily happiness.

... that lifestyle changes are necessary to live a balanced life.

... that beauty lies not in shape, hair or clothes, but in the openness of heart and the capacity for joyous laughter.

... that people who are truly happy have stopped trying to figure it all out.

... that people are ready to love us more than we generally allow them to.

... that promises are sacred.

... to embrace my weaknesses in order to attract someone who complements them.

... that freedom comes as a result of letting go, not holding on.

... that gossip will weaken any business as it spreads.

... that going home is not always a physical experience.

... that when I focus on a problem it will become bigger.

... that the more we embrace death the richer life becomes.

... that there is no such thing as common sense.

... that it is easier to accept feelings than it is to rationalize them.

... that what we are driven to get isn't always what we want.

... that a lesson only becomes a lesson when it moves us along our path.

... to trust my instincts – they are usually right.

... that it's okay to be serious.

... that the greatest power is the power of choice.

... that disappointment is directly proportionate to expectations regarding circumstances beyond our control.

... that my soul mate is my greatest teacher.

... that spending time daily in deep relaxation is not an option for personal growth, it's a requirement.

... that taking no action is taking an action.

... that most of the time we use words too cheaply.

... that the answer is indeed the question.

... that if you don't do everything you can right now, you'll have more to do later.

... that it's important, along the road to our dreams, to stop and re-examine the map just to make sure we haven't gotten lost.

... that we cannot change our reality until we ask better questions.

... that when we overprepare, our performance loses its authenticity and humanity.

... that learning is a lifestyle.

... that credentials on the wall do not make for a decent human being.

... that inspiration comes from the strangest of places.

I Have Learned...

   ... that health is the most important thing by asking those who no longer have it.

   ... that there are only two truths: life and death. Everything else really doesn't matter.

   ... that fear, when managed, promotes excellence and creativity.

   ... that the best games to play are the ones where I can make up my own rules.

   ... that when I am at my most vulnerable, I am most ready to grow.

   ... that self-worth isn't everything, it's just that there isn't anything without it.

   ... that sharing myself with others is the greatest gift I can ever give.

   ... that no one can ever love me enough if I do not love myself enough first.

   ... that spirituality is, in essence, about how well-connected we are to Self and others.

   ... that it is better to make a decision and find out it was wrong, than to avoid making any decision at all.

   ... that technology is simply a tool that can be used for good or bad.

   ... that I can learn and grow from everyone I meet.

   ... that serious people need love too.

   ... that the degree to which I engage with other people is the degree to which I participate in life.

I have learned that

regret lasts forever.

I Have Learned...

... that we always find time to do what is truly most important, even if we claim otherwise.

... that most problems are created out of boredom.

... that when I stop searching for something it really does show up.

... that regret lasts forever.

... that a compliment thought but not shared is a missed opportunity.

... that hiring the right people makes management unnecessary.

... that we are either fully engaged in the game of life or suppressed by it.

... that participation is the name of the game.

... that our perceptions are often colored by that for which we are looking.

... that people change when they want to change and not one moment sooner.

... that people will always do what they are rewarded for doing.

... that people who are constantly busy are often hiding from something.

... that sometimes it's best just to shut up and get over it.

... that the best coaches coach from their hearts, not just their minds.

... that most regrets come from the things I DIDN'T do.

... that problems come more from systems than they do from people.

... that our lives are about patterns.

... that living completely involves loving deeply.

... that a great business card does not necessarily represent a great business.

... that people who do not respect others do not respect themselves.

... that I always feel better after I get out of bed.

... that when I do not get what I want, it probably wasn't meant for me.

... that there are people who love us dearly but just haven't been taught to show it the way we want them to.

... that if I enjoy every day as perfect I will never have regrets.

... that career can be the elusive thief of true identity.

... that the wisest decisions are made with the counsel of the heart.

... that we want to hear the truth about ourselves, we should ask our families.

... that most of the things that made me feel happy when I was ten still do.

... that discovering life's best-kept secrets is as easy as asking someone who has just lost a loved one.

... that one way to understand something is to discern its complete opposite.

I Have Learned...

... that life doesn't have to make sense.

... that longing for the future can keep me from getting there.

... that people have difficulty asking for what they want.

... that motion, not contemplation, leads to success.

... that obstacles are visible only when I take my eyes off the goal.

... that life is disproportionately shorter at 40 than it seemed to be at 20.

... that my wife is usually right.

... that making peace with the past really does create freedom.

... that sometimes my daughter just wants me to say, "Hmmm," instead of giving her the solution.

... that love is something to do and not just a feeling.

... that nothing can make me happy except myself.

... that men seldom go fishing because they like eating fish.

... to embrace the beauty of silence, for therein lies the answers.

... that love is deeper when you give it, not when you get it.

... that even the most intense feelings and reactions will subside over time.

... that lightness is not the opposite of seriousness, it is the opposite of heaviness.

I have learned that people

change when they want to

change

and not a moment sooner.

I Have Learned...

   ... that if I never risk losing anything then I never really win.

   ... to ask my guardian angels for what I want and to thank them out loud.

   ... that the foundation of a great relationship is knowing how to love, trust and take great care of myself.

   ... that drinking good cappuccino with a good friend is a great way to heal.

   ... that it feels good to treat myself like company in my own home.

   ... that the more I give away, the less it and I are valued.

   ... that the human mind is like a parachute – neither functions until fully opened.

   ... that money is a lousy way of keeping score.

   ... that although I can't always get what I want when I want it, the Universe always provides what I need when I need it.

   ... that the main way to express love is to show attention.

   ... that limiting beliefs are usually supported by unmet needs.

   ... that inaction breeds stagnation. Stagnation stinks.

   ... that a full pipeline is the best insurance for long-term sales success.

   ... that if it has anything to do with money, get it in writing.

   ... that anything is possible if I can let go of my attachment to a specific outcome.

... that crying is not a sign of weakness but a catharsis.

... that anger is hurt turned outward.

... that every plan I make is useful only until I get to the next bend in the road of life's journey.

... that relationships are one of the most important and least understood arenas of human life; they can confine or liberate, suppress or inspire.

... that everyone enjoys a lollipop after seeing a doctor.

... that one of the most important keys to rapport is pronouncing everyone's name correctly.

... that if I pay attention to inklings and nudges, I can avoid problems and crises.

... that action is the antidote to fear and depression.

... that a good time to practice diaphragmatic breathing is during a long bus or train ride.

... that if we teach three-year-olds sophisticated, multisyllabic words, they won't be intimidated by the "big" words they encounter at fifty.

... that candid snapshots preserve a family's most magical moments.

... that sandals look prettier on pedicured feet.

... that today's risk is tomorrow's piece of cake.

... that sunset at the Grand Canyon is one of life's must-sees.

... that it takes years to build up trust, and only seconds to destroy it.

I Have Learned...

... that Auntie Olive was right when she said, "Nothing happens before its time."

... that golden moments shared with grandparents are remembered long after those grandparents are gone.

... that today's cuties are the hunks of tomorrow.

... that sometimes when I think I'm hungry, I'm really thirsty instead.

... that we can only care for others as well as we are caring for ourselves.

... that shoes are more comfortable on pedicured feet.

... that sex does not equal love.

... that people who are good at making excuses are good at little else.

... that people who think they're smarter than the rest of us aren't.

... that success is a poor teacher.

... that growing old gracefully is harder at 40 than it is at 20.

... that when something isn't clear it's time to ask better questions.

... that it's time to stop second-guessing myself and making excuses for others.

... that being a fast typist is much more useful than I imagined before becoming one.

... that children hate television when they're given better options.

I have learned that

anger is hurt turned outward.

I Have Learned...

... that just when I think I know what's going on, I inevitably get a kick in the butt from the Universe.

... that gratitude is the gateway to joy.

... that loving an under-appreciated person changes them forever.

... that genuine wealth resides within personal satisfaction.

... that it's okay to say "no."

... by paying attention to others' responses, that I am more attractive when I wear bright colors.

... that students and clients teach me as much, if not more, than I teach them.

... that all activities are more successful when I become mindful of the one's ending and the next one's beginning.

... that being defensive is oxymoronic – it usually invites stones to be thrown.

... that laughter can be self-generated, it doesn't always have to be in response.

... that sometimes "things" don't fit because I haven't grown into them yet.

... that sometimes people who mean to help can also hurt.

... that coaching isn't about holding clients accountable, it's about their becoming responsible.

... that it's important to define what I need as opposed to want I want.

... that once we get our needs met, we spend our lives being pulled forward, rather than chasing.

... that by next week, today's high drama will probably seem like just another minor event.

... that it's actually cheaper to eat healthfully.

... that if I drink enough water to pee clear, I will think more clearly.

... that I save money and calories when I pack my own bag lunch.

... that the more complex and psychological the angst, the more simple and visceral the root problem.

... that it's important to make love even when I think I'm too tired—sometimes especially then.

... that just when we think we are full, life gives us more to enjoy.

... that if we give children really good paints they will know you believe they have a masterpiece inside.

... that problems evaporate when I ask for solutions along with complaints.

... to receive my man's plowing the driveway as an expression of great tenderness.

... that giving extravagantly and to the point of foolishness makes God sing.

... that the person who knows all the names almost always has control of the situation.

... that of all my talents and skills, my faith is my most powerful strength.

I Have Learned...

... that speaking my truth doesn't always require words.

... that swimming upstream is a challenge as well as tiring.

... that people change for their reasons, not mine.

... that peace is of the mind, not the senses.

... that outlook determines outcome.

... that people need acknowledgment and endorsement far more than they need suggestions for improvement.

... that parents get smarter and more acceptable to children as the children become older than 21.

... that instead of being walls to keep people out, personal boundaries allow closeness without sacrifice.

... that everyone is my teacher.

... that if I remain true to myself, I cannot be anything but authentic with others.

... that huge mountains are climbed by taking little steps.

... that the Universe provides richly for those who are willing to receive and not block input.

... that we make programs work for us, instead of us working for them.

... that getting in the "flow" means literally firing up my entire brain.

... that there is no such thing as a straight line.

... to expect that what I see as absolute truth one day may seem completely ludicrous the next.

... to appreciate being able to go to a bookstore to read what's new, even if I don't buy anything.

... that it's best to learn from other peoples' mistakes and experiences.

... that even the most chaotic situations eventually reveal a pattern.

... that activities like vacuuming and dusting are essential to being an artist.

... that writing about something makes everyone assume you're an expert.

... that it's not possible to love someone too much.

... that we need to place our trust in ourselves before we place it in others.

... not to assume that people know what I haven't told them.

... that taking the boulders out of a stream makes it flow faster.

... that more options are better.

... that raising kids is like a marathon, only we don't get to practice before joining the race.

... that one of the key ingredients for a successful new business is a wide network.

... that the best ideas come to me when I'm engaged in an activity I love.

... that at a profound level the less I need, the more freedom of choice I experience.

I Have Learned...

... that for every opinion there is an equal and opposite opinion at almost any gathering of people.

... that all personal development practices boil down to the same few basic principles.

... that abundance is not received or owned, it is chosen.

... that proving worth is the ego's endless game of running in circles.

... that life gets easier when I do what I say.

... that our body screams the pain to which we don't give voice.

... that non-decisions plus time equal clutter.

... that no team succeeds if composed solely of similar players.

... that people have a need to be understood and respected.

... that sooner or later technology is going to catch up with me.

... that people do the best that they can with the tools they have.

... that not everything called "spiritual" really is.

... that being surrounded with people who bring joy is a form of extreme selfcare.

... that living my values has truly opened the way to the successful expression of my talents.

... that no matter what the consequences, those who are honest get further in life.

... that life is more wonderful when my inner child has a voice, a vote and her needs met.

... that I am incredibly grateful to my children for having children.

... that "too good to be true" deals usually aren't.

... that nine times out of ten, when I have a new idea it has already being done.

... that the beauty of the earth is ours to enjoy if we take time to enjoy it.

... that sugar is one of the most powerful drugs on the planet.

... that a mindless, boring, repetitive job can lead to a tremendous output of creative ideas.

... that I can do anything; the difficulty lies in choosing what that shall be.

... to appreciate the majesty of mountains, thunderstorms, prairies, canyons and bodies of water for "big" problems suddenly become minuscule in their presence.

... that it's far easier to adapt old lessons to new situations than to invent something new and untested for each situation.

... that the more I depend upon forces outside of myself, the more I am a slave to them.

... that I'd rather feel the full range of emotions than block out an opportunity to experience life at its fullest.

... that meditation grounds me when life feels like it's falling apart.

I Have Learned...

    ... that one of the great mysteries of our time is: which came first, science or spirit?

    ... that appreciating my partner's greatest traits is the key to long-lasting love.

    ... that if work isn't play, I'm in the wrong job.

    ... that the 30/10 rule really works. Commit 30 minutes to learning something new each and every day, then spend 10 minutes deciding how to apply it to life.

    ... that as a coach it is my job to see what's inside you and to help you express that.

    ... that many people say things at funerals they would never say in real life.

    ... that the celebration of Self is a high-octane, no-cost form of energy.

    ... that the opinions of others reveal more about them than about us.

    ... that I never regret waking my children up to see stars.

    ... that a little girl needs her daddy too.

    ... that the law of reciprocity applies in all areas of life.

    ... that the grass can be greener on this side of the fence – if it is cared for.

    ... that it's not so much where we are but in which direction we are moving.

    ... that if I find myself in a hole it's time to put down the shovel.

... that some of the most simple inputs have the most profound effect.

... that children absorb and reflect the energy that surrounds them.

... that an effortless life begins when I stop trying to create one.

... that a "missed opportunity" is really a choice that's still beyond awareness.

... that by identifying and eliminating expectations, I free myself to more fully receive.

... that driving a VW Camper Van is like inland sailing.

... that it's better to give than to receive, but only if I have something to contribute in the first place.

... that attitude either inhibits or empowers – it's my choice.

... that adversity is a most powerful refining force.

... that having pets keeps me human.

... that I can always find something for which I can be grateful.

... that I can have a whole day with nothing urgent.

... that awareness is the first step toward change.

... that honoring differences brings people closer.

... that the best way to be filled in an exchange with others is to empty my own ego at the door.

I Have Learned...

... that I always have joy available — it's up to me to recognize and experience it.

... to value hunches, intuition and my gut much, much more than logic.

... to appreciate the poetry of any sport played at a championship level.

... that having a personal appointment book and a "to do list" is of no use unless I read them.

... that I am worth loving.

... that "spiritual laws" are inherently paradoxical.

... that it's often easier to tell others what's wrong than to model what's right.

... that it is better to light a few candles than to complain about the dark.

... never to let anyone else determine how I feel.

... that conflict can be the first step toward reconciliation.

... that loving others is something I can choose to do even when I don't particularly feel like doing so.

... that having no choices is a choice that some people sometimes make for themselves and others.

... that it's better not to have problems than to solve them.

... that my morality is uniquely my own, inherently not shared by others.

... that the greatest aspect of me is not what I see in the mirror.

... that the opposite of community is loneliness.

... that love survives the grave.

... that all change takes place in the present.

... that competition is exhausting and cooperation is energizing.

... that two wrongs only lead to more of the same.

... that hearses never tow U-Haul trailers, because "you can't take it with you when you go."

... that giving up the Lone Ranger mentality allows others to provide support.

... that only God is forever; everything else is negotiable.

... that it's always worthwhile to be the first to introduce myself.

... that friendship is not an adequate basis for a business partnership.

... that taking away fear opens up the door to dreams.

... that spending just a moment acknowledging a child with our undivided attention does wonders for his self-esteem.

... that guilt is always about the past, anxiety is always about the future and either can destroy a perfectly good life in the present.

... that hard work, in and of itself, is not a crucial factor in getting results.

... that some battles are just not worth the fight.

I HAVE LEARNED...

... that those who have been labeled "great" or even "divine" have earned their reputation simply by daring to be fully human.

... that genuine worship happens not at the altar, but at the moment of joyful surrender.

... that depression is a symptom of not living life on your own terms.

... that even when it seems there's no more to give, a friend's cry for help creates the strength to help.

... that sometimes more loyalty comes from a pet than a relative or a friend.

... that delighting in paradox makes the mysteries of life much less painful.

... that happiness comes from giving.

... that everything we do takes longer and costs more than expected.

... that each of us is always doing the best we can, even when it seems otherwise to folks around us.

... that sexual infidelity is not the only way one can be unfaithful.

... that scrumptious doesn't always have to be unhealthy; healthy doesn't have to be dry and bland.

... that embedded in today's disappointments, defeats, and horrible mistakes are the seeds for tomorrow's serendipities, triumphs and strokes of genius.

... that if in doubt, don't say it.

... that every action has consequences and we ought to be ready for the payback, good or bad.

... that the Internet has changed everything about how we interact with our community and our economy.

... that boredom is the price we pay for being self-absorbed.

... that if you judge people you have no time to love them.

... that while there's no second chance to make a first impression, one can behave impressively in any situation.

... that changing habits on a deep level takes willingness, consistent application and time.

... that peace does not start "at home," but within every one of us.

... that running on adrenaline is like running on a battery pack. Eventually, power is depleted and life either needs to be recharged or discarded.

... that fear and that which we don't understand are one and the same.

... that even serious grownups need a cigar box full of little treasures.

... that the best coaches stay on the sidelines while the team reaps glory on life's playing fields.

... that offering items from a website requires willingness to ship around the entire world.

... that if you don't wear shoes shaped like feet, eventually your feet will be shaped like those shoes.

I Have Learned...

... that hugs say things when words are insufficient.

... that being honest eliminates trying to remember what was said.

... that the Universe is like a boomerang, throwing back at us whatever we intend with a force greater than our own.

... that you cannot lose control of that which you have never controlled in the first place – like another human being.

... to always question reality.

... that what is true on one side of town can be a lie for those who live on the other.

... that while it takes a village to raise a child, a single critic can undermine her self-esteem.

... that it's okay to say, "I don't know."

... to ask the professionals I hire whether they attended and were alert during the classes that pertain to my particular situation.

... that no matter what I learn, someone invariably learned it long before I did.

... that strangers are simply people who have many of the same hopes, dreams and challenges as do the people I already know.

... that being responsible sometimes requires a reminder that I am able to respond.

... to increase my own sense of gratitude by writing thank you notes on checks I send each month.

... that love is the universal antidote to fear.

... that "evil" is what occurs when we "live" in reverse.

... that for every hour spent in anger and worry, we give up an hour of peace of mind.

... that only I can determine the reality I face on a given day.

... not to wage war on too many fronts – to pick my battles and battlefield carefully.

... that a good haircut is always a good investment.

... that every bureaucracy was once a creative idea so valuable it deserved multiplication.

... that it's always easier to make a decision when all the information is available.

... that most human misery is a result of failure to take responsibility for one's own actions and situations.

... that being and doing are each necessary to living a balanced existence.

... that corporations do not make decisions. People within corporations make decisions.

... that all coaching is personal coaching.

... that genuine faith is not something I have, but is something that has me instead.

... that "No" is a complete sentence.

... that the basic goal of every religious system is personal fulfillment.

I HAVE LEARNED...

    ... that avoiding pain is ultimately more painful than facing it.

    ... that strong reserves are the best safety net.

    ... that either we control our attitude or it controls us.

    ... that anything and anyone can be worshiped. All that's required is ultimate allegiance.

    ... that relationships are built on agreements kept.

    ... that there is no separation between the sacred (or holy) and the profane (or secular). There is only one creation.

    ... that the only "primitive" thing about most ancient peoples was their technology, not their humanity.

    ... that adding value adds profits fast.

    ... that it's often more difficult to be than to do.

    ... that meditation helps me stay tuned to the wisdom channel.

    ... that life is not fair. Who said it was supposed to be?

    ... that organizations don't run on information, they run on relationships.

    ... that my children learn more from what I do than what I say.

    ... that mothers' mantras stay with their children for a lifetime.

    ... that listening for the whispered messages in life is more fun than waiting for all the shouting.

... that the biggest blocks to learning are the words "I know."

... that living in the same town I grew up in is nothing to be ashamed of.

... that no one likes to be told they're wrong, so make them right.

... that the world doesn't stop for anyone's personal grief.

... that love is the binding energy that connects all of us.

... that time and energy are far better spent delegating tasks to others than trying to strengthen my weaknesses.

... that progress is people demanding impossible things.

... that I can't tell whether my clients are happy — only they can.

... that a coach is to life as oil is to an engine — small regular doses keep everything running smoothly.

... that it's all good.

... that judgment always comes back to haunt us in the form of a situation that mirrors the one we have judged.

... that I can only begin where I am, not where I wish I were or think I should be.

... that health is wealth.

... that a half-truth is a full lie.

... that everyone has a peak performance time of day.

... that I am my best when I am my most natural, relaxed self.

I Have Learned...

... that coaches need coaches like dentists need dentists
– and everybody responds best to a pretty smile.

... telling the truth doesn't cause trouble, trouble comes
with not telling enough of the truth.

... that if you compliment children on good deeds they are
more likely to do them again.

... that more learning leads to more humility. Lack of
humility is really a sign of ignorance.

... that it is often true that whatever we resist is our
next best step.

... that there is nothing so frightening as the noise made by
a sharp mind debating itself.

... that making no choice is a choice.

... that the only problems we have to solve are our own.

... that people who confuse the Beatles with the Monkees
are now 30 years old.

... that a good night's sleep will resolve many issues.

... that before saying "yes" to something, it's important to
consider what "no" would mean.

... that chocolate does indeed take the sting out
of a bad day.

... that the love of my family always warms my heart.

... that change begins with a decision, grows with a
commitment and occurs with action.

... that the greatest path to travel along is the one I create.

... that a leader who is too far out in front tends to blend in with the horizon and lose effectiveness.

... that we will fly faster with less effort if we surround ourselves with those flying in the same direction.

... that every day is a great day to be alive.

... that a grateful heart sees the good in every living being and every action.

... that asking for help only works when we make space to receive it.

... that it's important to wipe your feet before you move on so you don't track yesterday's mud.

... that everyone has "stuff."

... that as a coach I see people in terms of future potential, not past performance.

... that children don't keep.

... that computers, like cars, are wonderful when they work.

... that cleaning out a closet makes space for more than just stuff for the closet.

... that love is a gift to the giver.

... that I don't have to see myself as not good enough, bad, or dysfunctional in order to grow and change.

... that animals are great judges of character.

... that spending 90% of life in the present will reduce the past to memory. The future will take care of itself.

I Have Learned...

... that when you raise your standards to express your values the world will line up behind your boundaries.

... that I can't talk my way out of a situation I lived my way into.

... that hot cereal tastes better with golden raisins and chopped walnuts in it.

... that everyone has failed at something and survived.

... that if chocolate ice cream has peanut butter in it, it tastes better.

... that I am most at peace and things work out the best when I give up my need for control.

... that I can decide to take the freeway or to go off-road, but to forgo planning the route is sheer folly.

... that the longer we take to be who we are, the longer it takes to get what we want.

... that dogs embody love, loyalty, compassion, forgiveness and trust, demonstrating these attributes without pride or the expectation of reward.

... that failure is the result of giving up.

... that everyone prefers to be held in an embrace rather than placed on a pedestal.

... that we can't NOT be on our path.

... that having passion for what I do changes how I see my environment.

... that when we misdirect the floodlight of attention it can, at best, illuminate where we have been; at worst, blind us to where we are going.

... that silly is good.

... that consultants get paid to learn; coaches get paid to grow.

... that giving it away is the only way to keep it.

... that dogs and most other things come more easily if they're not chased after.

... that delegating responsibility without accountability is a prescription for frustration and failure.

... that ebb and flow occur in all relationships and all aspects of life.

... that experience is the toughest teacher – she gives you the test first and the lesson later.

... that withholding is the perfect way to stay stuck.

... that it's okay to give lots of hugs even when they are not expected.

... that even though the sentence that will solve all my problems is probably written in a book, there's no guarantee I'll be concentrating when I read it.

... that brewpubs look exactly the same no matter what city or town they're in.

... that "walking your talk" is the only game worth playing.

... that unconditional love means more than mere acceptance of what is; it means SUPPORTING others as if they were already absolutely perfect.

... that if you are not sure what kind of work to do, finding out what you loved doing when you were 5 to 7 years old will put you on the right track.

I Have Learned...

... that I can't do everything.

... that it's foolish to hope, wish, or believe that someone will treat me better than they treated the person before me.

... that it's important yet difficult to distinguish between a blip in the data and the beginning of a trend.

... that during a crisis slowing down is the best action to take.

... that compassion is the path to loving someone who is hurtful.

... that the brightest stars in the universe pale in comparison to being truly in love.

... that every thought we think is a prayer and that all prayer is answered on some level.

... that action relieves anxiety.

... that alcohol postpones the sting of a bad day, but the sting gets infected and festers.

... that friendship is more enduring than passion.

... that endorphins are a much gentler, satisfying energy source than adrenaline and that both are addictive.

... that I interpret the world, so it exists as I see it.

... that I can reinvent myself – over and over if I want – but doing so is exhausting.

... that allowing love to grow will fill up all the empty spaces.

... that if I remember that when I feel fear I'm not the only one, I can release it more easily.

... that doing for others what they can do for themselves is not helping, it's crippling.

... that if I fail to say "no" enough, I run out of energy, my circuits overload and I shut down.

... that the best cure for feeling lonely is to touch someone else profoundly.

... that money and spirituality are an amazing combination.

... that I can say "no" and still give and receive love and support.

... that clients will pay whatever I am willing to receive.

... that everyone can add value.

... that daily focus creates reality.

... that our subconscious is the world's most outrageous computer and, as with all computers, it's garbage in, garbage out.

... that simply and continually putting one foot in front of the other allows miracles to happen.

... that when I thought I was being noble and "selfless," I was actually being manipulative.

... that when I follow my heart, a woman I respect shows up in the process.

... that a goal is merely an excuse for being in the process.

... that I am who I am, not what I do.

I Have Learned...

... that the true victory is in the process, not the end result.

... that imagination can find possibilities where there seem to be none.

... that failure is a gateway to a new level of self-acceptance and appreciation for the perfection of the Universe.

... that the only meaning in the world is that which we and God assign.

... that genuine wisdom comes only from life-experience, while knowledge comes from learning.

... that failure is often an illusion.

... that being single is better than being in an unfulfilling relationship.

... that as I give others freedom to be, I give myself freedom to be.

... to embrace the paradox that in stillness I may achieve my goals.

... that quiet is noisy to some people.

... that coincidences are simply miracles where God wants to remain anonymous.

... that when I give freely of that which I value, I receive tenfold back.

... that when push comes to shove, stop.

... that "Women Who Do Too Much" don't have to.

... that the key to a stress-free life is living in the moment.

... that worrying and figuring it out make life difficult, while having values and attending to our heart make it easy.

... that I want the 100,000 hours I devote to my career to be in harmony with the rest of my life.

... that children are not simply our future, but a vital part of the present as well.

... that it's easy to be myself and tough trying to be someone I'm not.

... that love doesn't always look the way I expect it to look.

... that wisdom is innate; it cannot be taught.

... that not everyone is coachable.

... that the only way to evolve is through the path of self-acceptance.

... that limits are imaginary.

... that people do things for their own reasons, not mine.

... that clutter gets in the way of me being my best self.

... that judgment and expectation drain energy.

... that a good coach tells bold-faced truths.

... that there are no teachers any more; we are all students, learning together.

... that comparisons are joyless.

... that friends almost always die when we don't expect it.

I Have Learned...

... that I can only give up controlling others when I am in control of myself.

... that many entrepreneurs rely on adrenaline for their energy, but that it is not worth the cost.

... that people have exactly what they are committed to having.

... that my vision is the path, my goals are the stepping stones.

... that love only has value in the giving.

... that life is full of mystery, with things we do not know and things we cannot know.

... that children teach me the lessons most challenging to master.

... that no amount of wishing it were so will make it so. Action is required.

... that life is a "quid pro quo" arrangement...to get more, we have to give more.

... that people struggle because they choose to struggle.

... that reality is based on perception.

... that an uncluttered environment creates more energy.

... that all people are a lot wonderful and a little strange in their own way.

... that competence is gained one domain at a time.

... that balance is transient and can never be taken for granted.

... that cheaters often prosper — temporarily.

... that I can and do create my own rules for playing the game of life.

... that not having a good time is a sign of not doing it right and, worse, missing the point entirely.

... that I accomplish more when I struggle less.

... that money will control me only if I allow it.

... that punching a pillow doesn't handle anger like having someone really listen.

... that whatever we focus on we give energy to.

... that if I had a tail, I'd wag it a LOT.

... that being selfish is a great investment.

... that reality is the same for everyone. What differs is only our individual perception of reality.

... that it's better to ask some dumb questions than to commit even dumber mistakes.

... that it's never too late.

... that attraction only works when I'm visible.

... that my true values are who I am.

... that God hears and loves even weary, uninspired prayers—sometimes, especially those.

... that compassion is being unafraid of what we see in other people.

... that people are their actions.

I Have Learned...

... that every change offers an opportunity.

... that happiness, success, or wealth is just a decision away, but energy management is a prerequisite for all these things.

... that what we tolerate saps our energy.

... that death is not a challenge – life is.

... that we are responsible for our own future.

... that if you continue to do what you've always done, you'll always get what you've always got.

... that the more empowered we are the more we can empower others.

... that choice gives power and fear drains it.

... that having to make sacrifices is the result of poor planning.

... that power is like love, the only way to have it is to give it away.

... that it is as selfish not to receive as it is not to give.

... that not all men come from Mars and not all women come from Venus.

... that flexibility is power and trust is eternal strength.

... that illness and weakness are both a challenge and an opportunity.

... that sailing to any destination involves being off-course 90% of the time.

... that being happy is a process not an end-point.

... that they do shoot messengers.

... how to invest my time rather than spend it.

... that the last judgment is when the last person on earth stops judging.

... that trust and confidence are built through empathy.

... that one of the best ways to help people is to create an environment in which they can help themselves.

... that God is a comedian, though few in the audience have learned to see the humor.

... that if it is not effortless we are probably doing it wrong.

... that good goal-setting requires a strong personal foundation.

... that if I need clients, they will feel my need rather than my value.

... that the quickest way to live in love is to conquer fear.

... that there are two possible outcomes in life — to have reasons why it didn't happen or to have results.

... that the object of life is to die young as late as possible.

... that I don't need to be Super Woman; it's enough if I am simply Super Me!

... that I love life.

... that if you do not know where you are going you will probably end up somewhere else.

... that followers must lead before leaders will follow.

I Have Learned...

... that nothing works from the top down.

... that I cannot change what I am not willing to face.

... that we do not live in a perfect world.

... that being effective takes less energy than being efficient.

... that having a reserve lends courage.

... that when I accept where I am in life, I move on to other places more effortlessly.

... that "faith" is a verb.

... that when I ask, "What can I learn today from this person in this relationship," I begin to love the person.

... that it is always worth the money to buy really good coffee.

... that being focused frees up more time.

... that a lot of things that seem important at the time really aren't.

... that an optimistic outlook consistently delivers good results.

... that when I believe in my own value, others are attracted to me.

... that when I live with intention but without attachment, amazing things happen.

... that Dorothy was right in the Wizard of Oz: our heart's desire usually is in our own backyard, but sometimes we have to travel far away to discover that.

... that when I act as a steward for my own gifts the
universe supports me in developing them.

... that each person's path is unique and often
undiscernible to anyone else.

... that simply observing people trying to control things is
more powerful than engaging them.

... that when I am clear about my values and needs, my
surroundings and community will support me.

... that "shoulds" are somebody else's standards
– not mine.

... that when I sit quietly my mind relaxes into my breath
and my spirit breathes.

... that "closing the sale" is really the beginning,
not the end.

... that when I feel lonely, it's because I am
disconnected from my own values.

... that knowledge is not enough; we must seek
understanding, wisdom, and mastery.

... that people, principles and results are important
– in that order.

... that spending an hour in nature can reveal the answer to
any human question we bring to it.

... that by planning my week I comfort my mind
with a structure in which to place all the changes
that will happen.

... that everyone responds to a smile.

... that the more thankful I am the more blessed I am.

I Have Learned...

... to stop on the threshold and breathe before entering a room, a relationship, a job or a group. This way I can sense how it feels for me and make a conscious decision to either leave or stay.

... to learn something from everything; even when I've hated how it feels.

... that the more I recognize my own uniqueness, the less I need to compare myself with others.

... that it's important to begin, then have faith I will know how to complete.

... that when I serve and give to others, I serve and give to myself.

... that every human being has a need to love, serve and create.

... that I am enough in the moment.

... that memory is notoriously selective.

... that life is wonderful, magical and beautiful, only to the degree we allow it to be.

... that only tasks can be managed; people must be led.

... that the best opportunities almost always come in disguise.

... that nobody ever gives me offense, I only take it.

... that life is a constant test on how to deal with others.

... that the more I "help," the more I remove personal power from others.

... that unconscious choice wins by default.

... that the only person I am going to be with forever
is myself.

... that relationships and judgments mirror how we feel
about ourselves.

... that freedom is a state of mind.

... that I can trust myself.

... that everything I need I already have.

... that a good groan, moan or sigh can feel great at times.

... that every person is a teacher and every situation
offers a lesson.

... that abundance is always the best perspective.

... that it's harder to play catch up than keep up.

... that a cynic is an idealist with an unfulfilled dream.

... that clearing physical space results in clearer
mental space.

... that good teachers don't tell everything they know.

... that when we know our values, no decision is difficult.

... that even the most outrageous behavior makes perfect
sense to the person doing it.

... that where there is worry, there is a struggle for control.

... that the greatest cure for personal stress is a satellite
photo of earth taken from space.

I Have Learned...

... that constant "doing" is a sign that our "being" is suffering.

... that if you ask a dumb question you get a smart answer.

... that the greater our sense of guilt, the greater our need to cast blame on others.

... that each of us sees and experiences the world uniquely.

... that if the price is too high — even if I can justify it — I must walk away from the deal.

... that when things start breaking or going wrong around me, it's a sign that I am out of integrity somewhere.

... that everyone behaves badly sometimes.

... that even The Energizer Bunny needs some time to recharge its batteries.

... that every dollar I receive will have come from some other person.

... that feelings cannot be dealt with by simply thinking about them. They must be experienced, acknowledged and accepted.

... that real love involves accepting people for who they are as well as who they aren't.

... that no one is better than me and I am no better than anyone else.

... that forgiveness is the key to joy.

... that I cannot always choose the circumstances I face, but can always choose how to react.

... that the laundry room is less crowded during the week.

... that the problem isn't important, it's how I handle the solution.

... that when I am overwhelmed it's time to call TIME-OUT.

... that I have to stop waiting for the "right" time and make the time right.

... that the most valuable gift we can give children is our enthusiasm.

... that most people just want to be heard.

... that my inklings are usually right.

... that life can be designed to be very, very simple.

... that my surroundings perfectly mirror the state of my internal environment.

... that silence between friends can be a precious gift.

... that the person shouting the loudest during a dispute is usually in the wrong.

... that there is no room in my life for enemies.

... that when someone says, "I told you so," I didn't hear them tell me.

... that the world will not end, no matter what I fail to do or what doesn't work out.

... that we never, ever stop learning.

... that in the absence of rules, people will make up their own.

... that crafting a life is not the same as "making a living."

I Have Learned...

... that my perception of "reality" is not shared by everyone.

... that it's always a good idea to know both the game and its rules before playing.

... that thoughts are things.

... that happiness is a choice more than a chance.

... that our thoughts create our reality.

... that success comes from doing what we love and loving what we do.

... that love speaks all languages.

... that of all the things I have, FUN is my very favorite.

... that a lifetime is too long to spend in any state short of bliss.

... that heaven is not a place, but a human condition.

... that personal space is more important than free time.

... that starting early creates a time reserve.

... that a million-dollar income begins with an active imagination.

... that telling the truth is the greatest liberator.

... that love is the best gift we can give to ourselves and others.

... that when I give thanks for what I already have I end up receiving more.

... that abundance is our natural state; lack is an illusion.

I have learned that the biggest

block  to learning are the words

"I know."

I Have Learned...

... that fear is one of life's biggest obstacles.

... to focus on solutions, not problems.

... that most people are really angels in disguise.

... that actually doing it is much less work than thinking about doing it.

... that money and success are the results of an open mind and a loving heart.

... that I am far wiser than I realize.

... that external problems have internal solutions.

... that the best way to learn anything is to teach it.

... that any hatefulness attributed to God originated in the human heart.

... that all talk about another that is not fundamentally constructive is just plain gossip.

... that we don't own our possessions, they possess us.

... that when we live our passion life becomes extremely satisfying.

... that it's important to avoid making our children the center of our lives.

... that it is a sign of true strength of character to be able to admit to making a mistake without excuse.

... that professionals succeed precisely as much as their clients succeed.

... that if creating something requires a great deal
of effort and struggle, it is likely not something I
should be doing.

... that my clients have all the answers within them, my job
is to hold the mirror.

... that nobody likes a smart-ass.

... that to truly appreciate poetry, I need to memorize it.

... that life is a dialog, not a monologue.

... that any great truth which cannot be stated simply is not
a great truth.

... that the greatest virtue is honesty.

... that sometimes the people you expect to kick you when
you're down will be the ones to help you get back up.

... that at the heart of all sin is dishonesty.

... that people don't pay for what they're given, they pay
for the value they perceive.

... that often all I can control in my life is my own attitude.

... that what counts is not what I have but who I have
in my life.

... that hating others takes a lot more energy than
acceptance.

... that listening is the most effective skill in coaching and
the hardest one to apply.

... that if I work for money, then I will never have enough.

I Have Learned...

... that if there's ever a hunch to trust, it's the one about making a back-up copy.

... that many people do not know what they really value.

... that most people already know the solutions, but need a coach to support what they know.

... that hiring a coach is an investment; the payoff depends upon shifts and actions I make myself.

... that clients who write down their commitments are much more likely to keep them.

... that my central job as a coach is to help my client establish new habits.

... that happiness lies within.

... that getting a "yes" doesn't always get us what we want.

... that employees must understand the employer's vision if the company is to succeed.

... that using history to explain present failures doesn't really work.

... that when you put a message out into the universe you can never tell how it will come back.

... that God loves me no matter what.

... to respect what I attract in my life.

... that in the quest for "perfect" we may sacrifice "good."

... that most tasks are easier when broken down into a sequence of smaller tasks.

I have learned that **failure** is the result of giving u p .

I HAVE LEARNED...

... that one of the greatest lessons we can teach others is how to laugh at themselves.

... that when I stop chasing happiness I have a much better chance of finding it.

... that much of life's frustration comes from thinking we need to be human "doings" when we are really human "beings."

... that truly loving and accepting myself is the first step in creating a mutually satisfying, long-term, intimate relationship.

... that we attract in others all that which we have not learned to accept in ourselves.

... that getting my needs met is an investment in personal power and strength.

... that simple living is a great adventure.

... that the words we speak create our reality.

... that life is far more than it is cracked up to be.

... that giving someone everything I want to receive won't make them feel nearly so loved as giving what they want to receive.

... that work can be as much fun as play.

... that financial independence is a goal; financial freedom is a state of mind.

... that knowledge can be learned with the mind but wisdom must be acquired through experience.

... that if I go a very long time without some contact with nature, my spirit feels flat.

... that the quest for "perfection" is inevitably disappointing.

... that having a couple of great dogs is not a bad addiction.

... that I learn by listening, not by hearing myself talk.

... that I'm not willing to change my path to make others lives easier; neither am I willing to ask them to change theirs for me.

... that unless we work toward what we want, we will forever be wanting.

... that sharing ourselves with others is the purist form of self-expression.

... that selfishness allows room for true generosity.

... that people in need sometimes need our help.

... that the quality of life can always be better no matter how well I'm living now.

... that we must work at being a blessing to others and what a fulfilling task that is.

... I don't know as much as I think I know.

... that deep roots are just as indicative of health as far-reaching branches.

... to talk less and listen more.

... that loving well means giving others what they need, not what I feel like giving.

... that I MIGHT succeed without coaching, but I WILL succeed with it.

I Have Learned...

... that we cannot provide for others what we do not have for ourselves.

... that as people attend to what they need, want, value and gain joy from, they learn to love themselves more.

... that coaches train people to pay very close attention to who they are and what they want.

... that truly listening is like being a sponge with a brain.

... that sometimes we just have to feel the pain when we feel it.

... that it's best to write the good news and tell the bad.

... that most things take more time than we think they will.

... that it's always a mistake to fall in love with a person's potential.

... that the greatest gift we can give another person is to allow him or her to contribute to our life.

... that nothing's too hard once I get started.

... that the Golden Rule of "do unto others as you would have done unto you" works well only for people who want the same things I want.

... that weather is neither good nor bad, it just is.

... that I cannot train anything to come to me by yelling because it did not come more quickly.

... that it feels good to be generous with compliments and praise.

... that the first step to getting others to respect rights and boundaries is to respect them myself.

I have learned that
simply and continually
putting one foot
in front of the other
allows miracles to happen.

I Have Learned...

... that being loving spreads more joy than simply loving others.

... that the true friend is the one who will tell me the truth and help me feel good about hearing it.

... that controlling myself is tough enough without trying to control others too.

... that while a guru may help me to hear the still small voice within, the one to listen to is the still small voice.

... that when we say there are four directions, we forget earthward and skyward.

... that love is more about contribution than consumption.

... that living lightly feels good.

... that my Dad could fix everything.

... that no matter how much we know, there's always something new to learn and always someone who knows more.

... that old t-shirts, sweatshirts and towels make great rags.

... that life opens opportunities for each of us; we choose whether or not to take action.

... that life is a play and I get to write most of the script.

... that going to either extreme often leads to total reversal.

... that almost any problem seems less serious if I breathe deeply and slowly while contemplating it.

... that beauty is all around me if I take the time to look.

... that over-responding to subtle events speeds up evolution.

... that I can be my best friend.

... that people judge us by our actions not our intentions.

... that writing down a list of pros and cons may not help, but it will prevent me from taking action without stopping to think.

... that the world changes little; it's our perception of the world that changes.

... that people who flaunt one attribute usually have little else to offer.

... that loyalty is subjective and that being explicit about my definition will allow me to find people who want to fulfill it.

... that focusing on strengths is better than strengthening weaknesses.

... that life brings something special and joyful each and every day.

... that children help us to become grownups.

... that grilled cheese sandwiches and tomato soup will turn almost any day around.

... to be easy on people and tough on issues.

... that giving what we love to give is always more successful than giving what we think others want.

... that in order to rise up I must first stand up.

I Have Learned...

... that I feel most fulfilled when expressing unconditional love.

... that avoiding commitments inhibits the fullest experience of life.

... that faith is easier to practice with experience, but that it's harder to practice with baggage.

... that I cannot make people love me. All I can do is be open to being loved. The rest is up to them.

... that no matter how much you care, some people will never care back.

... after a fire that I can live well without an entire office of "stuff" I previously thought was indispensable.

... that it's not WHAT I have in my life but WHO I have in my life that counts.

... that intention + attention = miracles.

... that I can do something in an instant that will give me heartache for life.

... that no matter how thin we slice it there are always two sides.

... that it takes a long time to become the person I've always wanted to be.

... that while reaction is instinctual, the ability to respond intelligently is the hallmark of the evolving soul.

... that it is more effective to listen with my ears than with my mouth.

... that I should always leave loved ones with loving words; it may be the last time I see them.

I have learned that

reality is based on
perception.

I Have Learned...

... that some people recharge through peace and quiet, while others are energized by groups of people.

... that regardless of how hot and steamy a relationship is at first, infatuation inevitably fades and there had better be something substantial to take its place.

... that heroes are those who do what must be done, when it must be done, regardless of the consequences.

... that a true friend is someone I can have a great time with doing anything or even nothing at all.

... that a friend is someone I can relax with.

... that even when I have a right to be angry, I don't have the right to be cruel.

... not to put off what needs to be said; tomorrow may be too late.

... that true friendship continues to grow, even over the longest distance. The same goes for true love.

... that just because people don't love me the way I want them to, it doesn't mean they don't love me.

... that even frustrated mothers beam when you refer to their children as "precious" or "angel."

... that maturity has more to do with experiences and what we've learned from them than the number of birthdays we've celebrated.

... that we should never chastise a child for dreaming big dreams.

... that friends, no matter how good, will hurt me once in a while and that I must forgive them for that.

... that if I am staring at my own navel I will not be able to see the stars.

... that fortune awaits those bold enough to REACH for it.

... that forgiveness from others is worthless unless I fully forgive myself.

... that while our background and circumstances shape who we've been, we are responsible for who we become.

... that two people's love for one another cannot be measured by whether or how much they argue.

... that sometimes you have to put individuals ahead of their actions.

... that fulfillment comes from living my values.

... that we don't have to change friends if we understand that friends change.

... that fun is the confirmation of our belief in joy.

... that no matter how we try to protect our children, they will eventually get hurt and we will hurt in the process.

... that there are many ways of falling and staying in love.

... that since we only get one body we must take good care of it.

... that to have a friend I must first be a friend and to make sure to befriend someone who can be a friend in return.

... that emotional safety is the soil in which love can grow.

... that our lives can be changed in a matter of hours by people who don't even know us.

I Have Learned...

... that writing, as well as talking, can ease emotional pains.

... that high maintenance friends and relatives drain my energy.

... that the people we care about are inevitably taken from us too soon.

... that although the word "love" can have many different meanings, it loses value when over-used.

... that every problem or challenge has a solution, just not the one we may want.

... that there's a faint but important line between protecting someone's feelings and standing up for what I believe.

... that integrity is the steadfast refusal to do anything I will dislike myself for having done.

... that if I do not take care of myself, others will – on their terms.

... to listen to my inner voice, which knows neither pride nor arrogance, to learn the truth.

... that I love my parents, even as I struggle to know them.

... that success is not taught in school.

... that attracting people is much easier than convincing them.

... that listening for meaning is more productive than listening for words.

... that bizarre is in the eye of the beholder.

... that life is a process of casting away fear after fear.

I have learned that
the quickest way to
live in love
is to conquer

fear.

I Have Learned...

... that how we spend our time is often how we spend our money.

... that if we get what we need we will have what we want.

... that receiving occurs in direct proportion to the amount of giving I do, be it of time, of help or of love.

... that I am always living in complete integrity when I am being 100% of who I am, wherever I am.

... that we sometimes spend massive amounts of energy to avoid facing the truth.

... that God feeds all the birds but he doesn't dump food in their nest.

... that I always do exactly what I want even when I don't like what I am doing.

... that when we refuse to struggle, we achieve more.

... that we already embody our full "potential," we just have to "be" it.

... that being present in the moment is a richer experience than any I may be chasing after.

... that even possessing the greatest product in the world does not guarantee business success.

... that saying "no" can feel really great.

... that natural light charges and centers the soul.

... that my attitude, at any moment, is ALWAYS my choice.

... that nobody wins every game every time.

... that others respond directly to my moods.

... that life reveals itself to us one frame at a time; we mustn't mistake the current frame for the whole picture.

... that letting go of the assumption of needing to know it all allows the freedom to explore and an opportunity to learn from people who model what we want.

... that life becomes more effortless when I ask for even more than I think I need.

... that money is like any other tool. It never works well when misused, any more than a hammer can serve as a saw.

... that being truly in the moment means that I can't, by definition, be disappointed.

... that people take credit for their happiness and blame others for their misfortune.

... that not everything disguised as education is worth learning.

... that generosity pays the giver even better than it does the receiver.

... that love and laughter create.

... that truth comes from the most simple sources.

... that joy is the universe's way of telling us we're on the right track.

... that the journey is forever.

... that truth breeds more truth.

... that forever can be just today.

I Have Learned...

... that better answers come from sitting in silence than from any amount of thinking or conferring.

... that the younger the child, the wiser.

... that play is the prayer of our inner child.

... that it's not my job to rescue everyone I perceive to be making a horrendous mistake.

... that just because I think something is REALLY funny, that doesn't necessarily mean I should say it.

... that by trying to be "right" we can sacrifice being happy and well-loved.

... to practice walking a mile in someone else's shoes.

... that lives and spirits can be regenerated with respect, deep listening, safety and love.

... that the monsters under the bed disappear when I turn on the lights.

... that leadership comes from the heart, management from the head.

... that Vision + Determination = Living my Dreams.

... that opportunities will not arise if I'm not ready.

... that improving any organization starts with changing the self.

... that a strong focus eliminates more obstacles than any problem-solving strategy ever could.

... that sometimes we have to go through some turbulence to get out of the clouds.

I have learned that the best

opportunities

almost always come in

I Have Learned...

... that everyone and every situation in our world has something to teach us.

... that in the middle of the road there's a white line and dead animals.

... that all I need to know – good or bad – will come to me.

... that true listening requires abandoning my own agenda.

... that our true purpose in this life is to serve.

... that we are always at choice, especially when we think we have no options.

... that just because I have a fantastic idea, it doesn't mean I have to do anything with it.

... that I have to start from a place of love and kindness in all I do.

... that experiencing success in life without a vision is as unlikely as navigating through the wilderness without a compass.

... that attraction takes less action.

... that being able to "put up with a lot" doesn't make me strong, it just makes me tired.

... that if I take good care of my clients, they will open doors I could never open by myself.

... that sometimes making a 180-degree turn creates better results than continuing to push harder in the same direction.

... that by shedding tolerations, I'm much better at living in the present and enjoying daily moments.

... that people are often suspicious of praise and
    acknowledgment, perhaps because we're brought
    up in such a critical world.

... that both time and people are impossible to
    manage. The only thing I can manage is action.

... to model the way I would like others to treat me.

... to value the child within.

... that we create our own destiny.

... that it's not what we do but the way we do it.

... that if goals have imagination and vividness they will
    become reality.

... to take the time to lighten up by 75% every day.

... to take at least one action toward my goal every day.

... that there is still so much more to be learned.

... that whatever I throw out returns like a boomerang and
    seems to return faster and faster.

... that our visions about what's possible change
    as we evolve.

... that our relationship to money is a metaphor for our
    relationship to everything else.

... that people create opportunities.

... that people are always doing their best, even
    when they aren't.

... that passion for your business may not be enough to
    increase the bottom line.

I Have Learned...

... that a great coach learns more from her clients than she teaches them.

... that as long as I am determined to "go it alone," I get to go it alone.

... that sometimes I need to ask for help before I get it.

... that YOURS is mostly O-U-R-S.

... that you don't have to read books to look for new ways to develop; the opportunities and the means are all around.

... that my happiness is my responsibility and your happiness is your responsibility.

... that lessons get harder the longer we keep from learning them.

... to "let go" more often, to choose surrender over struggle.

... that "mastery" is not a destination, it is a journey, a path, a way of life.

... to appreciate the power of appreciation.

... that I experience peace when I fully live in the present.

... that some people are givers, others are takers; everyone chooses to be either one or the other in each moment.

... that what we resist gains strength.

... that when we medicate the pain, we mask its true source.

... that questions and silence can speak a thousand words.

... that life's greatest riches are found in relationships.

I have learned that
every person is a
teacher and every situation
offers a lesson.

I Have Learned...

... to expect that others generally operate from a different paradigm than mine.

... that "the perfect human" is a contradiction in terms.

... that the amount of joy I can feel is limited only by the amount of pain I can feel.

... that when I consider everything to be an experiment, my attachment to the outcome disappears.

... that a successful ending is the beginning of something even bigger.

... that every moment, every breath truly is a gift from God.

... that it is worth the occasional pain to always love like it's never going to hurt.

... that peace flows silently underneath chaos.

... that when we decide to make a major change, the Universe will suddenly and inexplicably tempt us to stay put; that's how we know we're on the right track.

... that if I listen carefully, I may actually hear what is really being said.

... that real change comes from endings and beginnings.

... that coaching is all about adding and subtracting something to my client's life.

... that not only the divine, but also the devil is in the details.

... that creativity is like a faucet: if we judge an idea before it flows, we shut-off all the ideas behind it.

... that maturity is the ability to objectively and
     critically evaluate self.

... that spending one minute thinking about nothing is
     more difficult and more valuable than thinking about
     something.

... that taking myself lightly has added light years to
     my life expectancy.

... that hard work seldom leads to happiness.

... that the thoughts I hold in mind control my direction.

... that starting something new takes me into unknown and
     exciting territory.

... that when I judge others, I disconnect from myself.

... that it is highly realistic to expect miracles.

... that when I resist, I suffer.

... that "no" is just a two-letter word.

... that my dreams are worth accomplishing.

... that true love holds no conditions, no expectations
     and no limitations.

... that the people with whom I am in a relationship mirror
     my thoughts, beliefs and actions.

... to forgive myself again and again and again.

... that my problems are my teachers.

... that when I judge others, I am judging myself.

I Have Learned...

... that, as hard as it is to change myself, it would be impossible for me to change anyone else.

... that my spiritual side is always in bliss.

... that my words are the tools to build my success, but only if I act upon them.

... that my Mom knew all there was to know, but that I couldn't take her word for it.

... that a strong intention attracts success.

... that my life will always be a process of learning, growing and healing.

... that when I'm in the midst of fear, confusion and uncertainty God listens and answers me.

... that a hectic schedule often covers a deep fear of boredom.

... that habits are like children, fighting with them is pointless. What they need first and foremost is love and acceptance.

... to trust my own wisdom even when it doesn't seem to make any sense.

... that things really are what they seem, but we can only comprehend that when we're seeing and listening skillfully.

... that absolutely anything can be communicated without hurting the listener, if enough love and skill are applied.

... that there is no illness that is not related to a choice between love and fear at some level, at some time.

I have learned that
what counts is not
what I have but who I have

in my life.

I Have Learned…

… that lessons come in layers like an onion. Peeling away those layers closest to the center take more focus, care and energy.

… that personal integrity resides beneath the layers of ethics and morality we frequently wrap around it.

… if we never say "no" our "yes" lacks worth.

… that more information does not give me a better life until I act upon it.

… that a smile or a gentle touch is often more satisfying than anything I can say.

… that being ill is not a sign of being bad, it is just a painful reminder that balance and well-being are more fun.

… that in order to give without depleting myself I have to double-check my reserves.

… that being happy is a simple goal that we make extremely difficult to achieve.

… that I don't have to worry in order to care.

… that the greatest enemy of "best" is "good enough."

… that I can validate my own experiences even when nobody shares them.

… that "doing the right thing" can take countless different forms, but invariably involves coming from the right place.

… that enjoying money and managing it well is a highly underestimated skill.

... that health is the absence of factors that inhibit balanced flow.

... that we either maintain or disrupt our health moment by moment.

... that we can always change our minds, even when doing so seems completely out of the question.

... that the way we label a situation reflects or can shift our perception of it.

... that we all are followers of one kind or another.

... that we are far less special and far more special than we think.

... that children teach us all that we need to know.

... that growth looks more like an EKG than a ski jump.

... that if I am content within myself everyone around me responds positively.

... that marriage evolves over time and that adjustment is ongoing.

... that a smile is a powerful way to communicate.

... that there are no coincidences, only invitations to enrichment.

... that manipulating or pretending never achieves as much as telling the truth about how I feel.

... that asking someone for help not only gets me help, it improves our relationship.

... that people value me to the extent I value myself.

I Have Learned...

... that everyone has something to offer; it's up to us to find the gift.

... that success is a by-product of living in the moment.

... that time is energy.

... that we are a gift to ourselves just waiting to be opened.

... that no two people see life in exactly the same way.

... that in personal growth, as in nature, there are no straight lines.

... that our inner light is never extinguished, just sometimes obscured by the haze of confusion.

... that saying "I'm sorry" is a sign of strength if I mean it; of weakness if I'm just trying to stave off the consequences of what I did or said.

... that life is a classroom and we are always the students, sometimes the teachers.

... that only when we surrender our ego can we discover our true selves.

... that the only way to experience true joy is to surrender completely.

... that it is not what happens but how we respond to what happens that will determine happiness and prosperity.

... that the Universe always gives us exactly what we need when we need it.

... that there is only today; tomorrow is just an idea.

... that truth energizes.

... that if I'm not getting the right answers, I'm asking the wrong questions.

... that the best parents learn more from their children than their children learn from them.

... that if I never speak my mind, I will eventually lose it.

... that satisfied customers are the wealth of any company.

... that we are all connected through invisible threads and if we pull one thread irresponsibly, we can unravel the whole cloth.

... that when we judge others, we are really judging ourselves.

... that we are sometimes the last ones to know ourselves.

... that when you follow your dreams they come true.

... that I am constantly forgetting most of what I have learned.

... that to make a speech, I have to fall in love with the audience; fear and love cannot occupy the same space.

... to stop being a victim of opportunities.

... that boldness is not enough for a successful presentation; preparation is essential.

... that when I lose interest in an activity, the need that activity met is now filled.

... that my eleven-year-old is smarter, but not wiser, than me.

... that rain on the roof presents a symphony to my heart.

I Have Learned...

... that lessons are repeated until they are really learned.

... that our best contacts come from unexpected sources in unexpected places.

... that I have more to learn from every person I will ever meet than I will ever know.

... that when we give of ourselves, the gift returns to us.

... that there are many ways to win that don't cost anyone anything.

... that we don't make friends, they make us.

... that all the true human stars have a twinkle in their eye.

... that when we stop chasing our dreams, they have a way of catching us.

... that it is by watching people that we can see ourselves.

... that when my mind and body walk the same path, the journey is wonderful.

... that smiling changes the very chemistry of our cells.

... that my feet will take me where my heart wants to go.

... that when the present is perfect, the past sneaks out the back door.

... that when we are "present minded" the past becomes "absent minded."

... that it's worthwhile to ruffle someone's feathers if in the end it helps them learn how to fly.

... that smiling opens the mind.

... that people who appreciate value will pay premium rates.

... that quality service attracts high paying customers.

... as many good things as bad things from my parents.

... that I am not my business; my business is but one expression of me.

... that I need not be ashamed of being depressed.

... that what I say is not necessarily what anyone hears.

... that family can make or break us.

... that children are the greatest teachers.

... that knowledge is pointless unless it inspires action.

... that being right is sometimes more important than being happy.

... that there is no answer, but that doesn't stop me from searching.

... that the ways others see us are often radically different from the way we see ourselves and that both ways are right.

... that learning one new thing every day expands the entire world.

... that we cannot truly give until we have learned to receive.

... that people will always surprise me.

... that whenever there's a lot of energy in a situation there is a big lesson to be learned.

I Have Learned...

... that attachment to a specific outcome is an attempt to buy security for the price of chance.

... that being a coach without a coach is like being a magician without a trick.

... that if I speak from my heart, my audience will hear from theirs.

... that growing a business requires not only working "in" it, but also "on" it.

... that silliness can shatter heavy thinking.

... that coming from the heart is never wrong.

... that maturity can be measured by how little delay there is between any stimulus and the appropriate response.

... that the word "but" negates all that preceded it; I use "and" instead.

... that a good marriage depends more upon being the right spouse than upon having the right spouse.

... that sometimes a permission slip is all we need.

... that a future full of possibilities is more attractive than a past full of accomplishments.

... that I would rather be close to my loved ones than to establish that I am "right."

... that it is impossible to love children and worry about them at the same time.

... that the only thing at which I can consistently succeed is the act of being myself.

... that my value is not in what I do but in who I am.

... that truly hearing another is as much fun as being heard.

... that I do not always amuse everyone around me and that's okay.

... that our children are affected by our moods.

... that pride tastes bitter if you do not swallow it.

... that most of our time is probably being spent just getting by.

... that my inner child is left-handed.

... that my way is right for me, not for everyone, darn it.

... that all is well, even when it seems as if the sky is falling.

... that it's easier to be funny out loud than it is to be in writing.

... that people stumble over their own feet more often than they do over others.

... that the path of least resistance is the fastest way to reach the destination.

... that all life experiences, both good and bad, earn positive interest over time.

... that when I smile, others smile back.

... to ask myself the same questions I would ask of others.

... that no matter what people say, they will do exactly what they want.

... that the way to change others is to change myself.

I Have Learned...

... that everything I have spent a lifetime learning is useless unless I continue learning.

... that my grandchildren have all the answers.

... that the way to get there is to go there.

... that moving forward is easy when I step out of my own way.

... that cleaning out the past makes room for the future.

... that we can be happy or we can be sad. I choose to be happy.

... that I receive respect when I give it.

... that sometimes the best way to change is in very tiny increments so that I barely notice it happening.

... that the strongest position I can hold is my own truth.

... that young people need to see a model of the type of adult they want to become.

... that one of the greatest treasures we can obtain is a clear understanding of our personal gifts.

... that when two people disagree, the quickest resolution comes when one of the two decides to hear the other completely.

... to always let truth lead the way because it will, whether I follow it or not.

... that once we "get" a message it becomes part of us.

... that when we stop looking for answers, the best questions appear.

... that the way we nurture our health reflects how we feel about ourselves.

... that worry is a waste of time and energy.

... that clients are brought into our lives so we can grow with them.

... that clients provide us an opportunity to share our gifts.

... that it's important to take the care to respond rather than react.

... that a client's trust is an honor to be won.

... that my choices either nourish or drain my energy.

... that who we are is more important than what we do.

... that every accomplishment adds to personal equity.

... that love is learning how to "be."

... that marriage can be the greatest gift if the right spouse is involved.

... that family is not limited to blood relatives.

... that knowing God is knowing truth.

... that shedding possessions makes room for more joy.

... that sex is often an excuse NOT to get intimate.

... that children sometimes mirror our behavior back to us in delightful and frightening ways.

... that what we learn in the moment helps us grow.

I Have Learned...

... that time is a gift to each of us.

... that when I feel complete as a person, I am "being," not "doing."

... that sharing my gifts is my life purpose.

... that self-care is a full-time job.

... that the more I learn, the more I realize how little I know.

... that we can't hear in others what we haven't listened to in ourselves.

... that reflecting back what I have heard others say gives me the space to take more risks when communicating.

... that at frenetic speeds the still, small voice of spirit is muted by the whirlwind of activity.

... that as a coach, my clients' lives are my product.

... that positive thoughts and actions bring positive experiences.

... that nothing is ever as scary as we feared it would be.

... that the most important things we say on any given day are those we say to ourselves.

... that allowing this moment to be perfect positions us best for the next moment.

... to never dismiss a goal before taking at least the first step toward achieving it.

... that where you are right now is where you are supposed to be.

... that by asking the right questions, we honor a
client's knowing.

... that the best feedback is both subjective and descriptive.

... that unmet needs blind us from values.

... that fear is a sign that something is missing.

... to accept that what is, is.

... that there is a link between my greatest strength and my
worst weakness.

... that true wisdom combines experience, knowledge
and intuition.

... that when I was acting outside of my integrity,
I was a real jerk.

... that learning is more fun than "knowing."

... that "knowing" renders "learning" impossible.

... that the truth is the most attractive thing of all.

... that one's true self can be deeply hidden.

... that the journey of self-discovery is a painful,
worthwhile adventure.

... that too much work can rob us of life.

... that like magic, a well-run start-up business becomes a
success during year three.

... that holding a newborn baby is way of experiencing
God's love.

I Have Learned...

... that the most important relationship each of us has in this life is with Spirit.

... that in relating with children, there is only the present moment.

... that compiling a list of what's wrong with religion is not a path to spirituality.

... that by asking "why," "what," "how" and "what if" about any situation usually uncovers some overlooked gem and that everyone has a blind spot around at least one of these questions.

... that "failure" can describe an outcome, but can never define a person.

... that all my problems started out as good ideas.

... that the best way to find a lost object is to start from where it was the last time I saw it.

... that no amount of business knowledge or experience is more powerful than simply testing what the market wants.

... that living life from the heart is much more fulfilling than living life from the head.

... that what I dwell on, grows.

... that happiness cannot be created, it is simply to be recognized.

... that all that stands between us and happiness is ourselves.

... that a great coach can hear what's going on with a client by changes in the client's breathing.

... that there is no place for sarcasm in coaching.

... that people only "hear" what they are ready to hear.

... that since we create our own games we might as well set
ourselves up to win.

... that when a client ends the relationship it's always
for the best.

... that the most direct, yet not the easiest, way to better
health and well-being is to eliminate toxic relationships
and break destructive habits.

... that the longer a habit has been held, the more time and
energy is needed to break it.

... that when we are quiet enough to listen, we are our own
best teachers.

... that everyone's way of receiving information is different
and a good teacher, coach or mentor will take the time
to learn the best approach.

... that our ability to authentically love others is in direct
proportion to our ability to authentically love ourselves.

... that learning to forgive takes practice.

... that there is always time for what we truly value.

... that nothing is free. Everything has a price.

... that we always attract others at a similar stage
of development.

... that relationships should and can be easy.

... that the level of peace I feel is dependent upon my
regularly spending time "just being."

I Have Learned...

... that fear will pass through quietly if I do not engage it in conversation.

... that the only exhausting thing about fear is hiding from and avoiding it.

... that creativity is stimulated by silence and stillness.

... that everything happens for a reason and a purpose that will serve us, either now or in the future.

... that worrying does not help.

... that the more I give, the more I get.

... that money is just money.

... that being good to myself is one of the best ways to be good to others.

... that trust starts with me being trustworthy.

... that the quality of life is determined by the quality of communications.

... that as we ask, so we receive.

... that problems are really divine opportunities.

... that people I view as "difficult" are actually teachers sent to help me evolve.

... that learning doesn't end until life does.

... that gifts are meant to be shared.

... that the only way to start is to start.

... that silk underwear is worth the money.

... that love and joy are both created by a decision to experience them.

... that a day without laughter is almost as bad as a day without prayer.

... that in a disagreement, seeing the other's perspective is even more satisfying than prevailing.

... that choosing to love unconditionally is sometimes a stretch, but it is the most valuable gift to give another - or self.

... that when I feel like I am off track, it's usually because my prayer time has been neglected.

... that there is enormous strength in gentleness.

... that the Bible is the best instruction book for life.

... that learning is just as much about integration as it is about intellect.

... that every expectation is a losing bet on an uncertain outcome.

... that ideas put into action create new realities.

... that anything seems possible when love for it exists.

... that love always heals, regardless of the pain's source.

... that reaching out to others brings joy.

... that in true peace, fear does not exist.

... to live fully, moment by moment.

... that ideas pause in our minds like butterflies.

I Have Learned...

... that the spirit of God is always with me.

... that Spirit comes to counsel me when I am
quiet and open.

... that taking ourselves too seriously makes life hard;
laughter makes it easy.

... that the more receptive I am to learning, the more
effortlessly the teachers appear in my life.

... that self acceptance is the foundation of receiving.

... that sharing is a spiritual way of life.

... that time reserves eliminate deadline crises
from one's life.

... that I always have a choice, even when circumstances
seem to be inflexible.

... that I design the mosaic of my life.

... that my life is perfect for me, even when I don't
understand why or how.

... that patience with myself and others allows growth.

... that the experience of love shared with a soul mate
exceeds description.

... that each succeeding step is easier to take than the first.

... that any first step often requires a leap of faith;
subsequent steps feel like old friends.

... that nothing is warmer than my husband's old sweater.

... that two slow, deep, focused breaths can restore
my peace of mind in any situation.

... that each of us has wisdom to share.

... that I can change my thoughts at any moment to focus on the positive.

... that every choice contains a moment of personal freedom.

... that every experience contains a truth.

... that I can choose to live with limited perspectives or to create new truths.

... that allowing other people's opinions to influence me usually limits my actions and growth.

... that life flows much more effortlessly when I take action sooner rather than later.

... that my spiritual center is my authentic Self.

... that happiness is both fleeting and ever-present.

... that the simple decision to be profoundly grateful for everything smoothes the path of life.

... that what I resist really does persist.

... that trusting what Life presents to me is always, ultimately, in my best interest.

... that the present is a gift.

... that listening to my heart is the wisest way for me to choose and decide.

... that my clients as a group are perfect mirrors of me.

I Have Learned...

... that after 10 years in business, founders or owners start looking for the right successor, even if they're not planning to retire for another 10 years.

... that we tolerate far too much.

... that although few people have learned how to design their own lives, anyone can.

... that everyone develops an ego and reactions in order to survive childhood.

... that my parents did the best they could, even if it was woefully inadequate.

... that having enough money is vital to peace of mind.

... that when enough value is added to the right people, success is guaranteed.

... that we were each handed a definition of success; if we are ever to feel successful we must redefine it for ourselves.

... by achieving it that outward, material success is overrated.

... that goal-setting can be deadly; better to over-respond to events.

... that success happens more easily when you are influenced by the right people.

... that singing silly songs need not be reserved for the young.

... that we can increase the occurrence of synchronicity and serendipity by eliminating the energy drains.

... that success does not depend on what I know, but on what others think of me.

... that at some point, we will stop pushing ourselves to grow and simply enjoy life.

... that as we mature we become more of who we were as a child.

... that some say love is the absence of fear, but I say that love occurs in the absence of need.

... that we are naturally pulled forward if we surround ourselves with people who bring out our best.

... that everybody needs something and if they think you have it, you probably do.

... that life can be about you, them, or it. Pick one and make sure you know which one you've picked.

... that a change of setting can transform a character flaw into strength.

... that our greatest gift is probably what's most obvious to others and most invisible to us.

... that being true to oneself actually requires less energy than self-deprivation.

... that we make decisions in nearly every moment, most of them unconsciously.

... that each past experience was essential to this moment in time.

... that when we are whole we can give freely.

... that people have more talent than they know what to do with.

I Have Learned...

... that "What if..." questions, asked after the fact, never yield a good answer.

... that children know what is really important in life.

... that building a successful person leads to building a successful business.

... that everyone is brilliant in some way.

... that my work is my love made visible.

... that parents always do the best they can, but that every family is "dysfunctional" anyway.

... that people meet our expectations - expect more, get more.

... that chitchat is how some people connect at a deep level.

... that most people take their talents for granted.

... that power is the ability to act.

... that nothing tastes better than a good piece of candy.

... that my husband of 24 years still excites me, ignites me, delights me.

... that our lives are the sum of our choices plus grace.

... that we experience less disappointment once we get that everyone makes decisions based on self-interest.

... that only people say "no." The Universe does not say "no."

... that I can consciously accelerate my own personal evolution.

... that not everyone wants to be inspired.

... that there is no "worst thing."

... that successfully dealing with loss is the same as
successfully dealing with life.

... that when God closes a door, He opens a window.

... that during intense crisis, it works just to do
the next thing.

... that to move forward in the world, we must give away
our knowledge.

... that if I'm talking, I'm not listening.

... that the greatest human need is to be heard
and understood.

... that gathering massive quantities of information doesn't
mean I'm learning.

... to measure success by living a great life.

... that seeking spirituality is not necessarily the way
to find it.

... that momentum is a much more sustainable personal
energy source than adrenaline.

... that if I don't love and take care of myself, I cannot
expect others to do so.

... that behind all hostility there is FEAR. When I reduce
fear, hostility goes away.

... that I haven't always learned my lesson.

... that the more I do, the less I get done.

I Have Learned...

... that credibility is proportional to distance: the farther I must travel to give advice, the more that advice is valued.

... that when we give expecting something in return, both we and the recipient are diminished.

... that the more I charge, the more I am respected.

... that the higher the quality of corporate coaching, the greater its acceptance in the organization and vice versa.

... that it's impossible to motivate another person; motivation happens from the inside out.

... that coaches, like cops, should ideally work their way out of a job, but given the nature of things, probably never will.

... that laughter makes life fun.

... that my judgments, opinions and stories don't make any difference because they don't change anything.

... that if I want to know what I truly want in life to look at what I have right now.

... that people who are proud of being selfish are less self-centered than people who try to avoid appearing selfish.

... that beating my opponent doesn't mean I've won.

... that everybody has in life exactly what they truly think they deserve.

... that if we really want to learn all about ourselves, we should create a list of everything we dislike in others.

... that we can not control our feelings, but we can control our attitude.

... not to do spirituality, but rather to be spiritual.

... that I need the support of peers before I challenge
    my superiors.

... that consensus helps the boss make her own decision.

... that this is the only life I have to live.

... that we all develop daily.

... that being unconditionally constructive makes me feel
    good about myself.

... that at times even liars speak the truth.

... that once you write something down it's more likely to
    be accomplished.

... that it is important to think big while taking consistent
    small actions.

... that some failures I cause and can correct; others are an
    inevitable part of life.

... that simply telling the truth creates a shift.

... that creating something new is a messy process.

... that our families want what's best for us, they just don't
    know what that is.

... that we are not expected to know how – we've never
    done this life before.

... that setting strong boundaries around space takes the lid
    off creativity.

... that we all fail a certain number of times before we suc-
    ceed; that number is concealed from us.

I Have Learned…

… that our bodies and minds are like cordless phones – they work best when they've been recharged.

… that not everyone who says they are ready for change is ready for the results change brings.

… that to create a new possibility, convene a group of people and give away the best ideas.

… that we're better off strengthening strengths and delegating weaknesses.

… that we have the freedom to choose.

… that doing my own thing makes me look powerful.

… that a coach without a coach is like a dentist who doesn't brush her teeth.

… that people are survivors.

… that we use our power every day without realizing it.

… that people want to help people.

… that the second "no" is one more step closer to a "yes."

… that people are motivated by either pain or pleasure. We move either away from or toward something with every action.

… that words are the least effective form of communication.

… that most people want to be inspired.

… that people are always searching for more.

… that there are some things we will never understand.

... that to change the world, I must change myself first.

... that the most important relationship in my life is the one I have with myself.

... that perfection means no more growth is possible.

... that the platinum rule is even more precious than the golden rule: do unto others as those others would have you do unto them.

... that chaos can serve us; it's one means through which we grow.

... that my friends reveal the type of person I am.

... that fighting is a senseless energy drain.

... that when I started trusting myself, others came to trust me.

... that patience reveals all.

... that it's not how great a product or service I have but how well I market that product or service.

... that my life and my world are a reflection of my thoughts and beliefs.

... that those who charge more are usually worth it.

... that silence is the greatest teacher, one that most people never meet.

... that "No" doesn't mean no, it just means not right here, or now, or in this way.

... that people are mean, people are rude, people are kind and people are wonderful.

I Have Learned...

... that the best tax break in the United States is to start your own business.

... who and what God is, and ... that I can't teach anyone this.

... that it's at the toughest times that we have the greatest breakthroughs.

... that people will help, if asked.

... that needing a partner's help often turns projects into disasters.

... that it only takes the moment at hand to make a change.

... that forgiveness of myself and others is essential to healing.

... that running from life won't make it go away.

... that we do grow out of our current friends – unless they grow too.

... to live in harmony with the world, rather than trying to master it.

... that most people can be good at most things, given determination, training and support.

... that real strength comes from within, not from dominion over others.

... that wisdom is not something learned, rather it is something that life creates.

... that once we understand how to live, life becomes easy.

... that people will only listen to me if I speak.

... that my job on earth is to live my life fully.

... that we are responsible for putting back into ourselves that which life takes out.

... that when we take decisive action, we often reap more than we originally set out to get.

... that my parents and teachers all turned out to be human.

... that money is nothing more than an exchange of energy.

... that the body often mirrors what's going on with mind and spirit.

... that people I deeply care for will disappoint, but that it won't sting as much if I recognize this inevitability.

... that it's not how much we know, but how quickly we learn.

... that tolerations are better teachers than monks or mystics.

... that the physical Universe never lies.

... that the Universe will keep repackaging the same message until I open it.

... that life is not long enough for any of us to perfect our weaknesses.

... that it's all just a game anyway.

... that there are always worthwhile lessons to learn from everyone.

... that simply being here now is a viable first step to solving most problems.

I Have Learned...

... that wisdom comes with maturity, not age.

... that my relationship with myself determines the quality of my relationship with others.

... that if I give much more than I expect to receive, I will get much more than I will ever need.

... that we learn more from our children than we will ever teach them.

... that becoming more selfish is the greatest gift we can give to those we love.

... that to acknowledge, claim and express Self is the only real task.

... that we generally see what we think we will.

... that events, relationships and belongings have the meaning we assign to them.

... that I can always choose peace instead of this.

... that since change is inevitable, I may as well choose to enjoy it.

... that we must make at least one life-threatening decision per year, just to feel at a cellular level just how important life is.

... that now is all we ever really have.

... that what I'm attracted to is not always in my best interest.

... that a period of doing nothing in silence can be the most productive time of the day.

... that making a tough decision is easier if I project myself into the future and imagine how I would like to recall the way I handled the situation.

... that no two opposing beliefs can occupy the same mind at the same time.

... that there's no such thing as a "false" hope.

... not to be afraid to ask for help.

... to focus on what can be controlled and to forget the rest.

... that what I get depends on what I am willing to give.

... that what each of us sees as "reality" is simply perception.

... that we usually get exactly what we expect to get.

... that the amount of time it takes to find a lost object is proportional to the level of agitation over misplacing it.

... that any couple has a greater chance for happiness together if they never have to share a sink, a closet or a toilet.

... that "giving up" is exactly that — handing struggle over to God.

... that "home" consists more of who we are and what we've brought than where we rest each night.

... that daily planners do not illustrate the value of a day.

... that action builds momentum.

I Have Learned...

... that when I let go of one trapeze it's good to float a bit before grabbing another one. The in-between place lets me know I can fly on my own for while.

... that I often get what I truly think I deserve.

... that when I don't take my purse out on a date with my husband I get to feel like I'm off-duty.

... that we can only move from where we are once we accept where we are.

... that today's problems can't be solved with yesterday's solutions.

... to always try just "one more time."

... that when I take responsibility for getting my personal needs met, the temptation to judge others disappears.

... that I can't "manage" another person's behavior, only my response to their behavior.

... that the power of choice determines the quality of life.

... that the wisest people are not those who write best sellers or who talk to sold-out crowds.

... that we all have the same amount of time.

... that criticizing what cannot be changed is a waste of time and energy.

... that when we take time to renew and rejuvenate, we have more energy to give others.

... that loving things are best said today and hurtful things better held until I forget.

... to stop asking people for what they cannot give and be content with what they can give.

... that when I'm blocked, I'm usually in the way.

... that it's always better to ask because the worst they can say is "no."

... that when I discount others, I discount myself.

... that we create our own luck.

... that wealth is no substitute for warmth.

... that if I do the hardest task first, the rest will be a snap.

... to look for actions that prove the words.

... that in the game of life, a sense of humor beats soul-searching angst every time.

... that what we think of as our unique precious personality is a cluster of random and mostly unconsciously adopted habits.

... that we do not "find" ourselves; we create ourselves.

... that I have to clear out old ideas periodically to make room for new ones.

... that there is MUCH more to wealth and success than money.

... that we are responsible for what we do, no matter how we feel.

... that to move forward I must take the first step.

... that we make the best use of opportunities once we stop thinking about all that could go wrong.

I Have Learned...

... that my balloon will rise when I cut loose the "baggage."

... that there might be a "right" way, but there is definitely no "wrong" way — except avoiding any action while waiting to discover the "right" one.

... to not stop with the first "right" answer.

... to savor the moment.

... that being successful is not necessarily the same as being happy.

... that when I accept others for who they are now they are more likely to grow.

... the power of the smell of bacon frying.

... that when I leave the house five minutes late I encounter mostly red lights; when I leave the house five minutes early I encounter mostly green lights.

... that what I can do is different from what I want to do.

... that the purpose of school is almost never spoken - to assist people in having meaningful, productive, joyous, contributory lives.

... that we teach people how to treat us by what we accept, not what we say.

... that truth resonates in the body like a radio frequency resonates in a stereo receiver.

... that unhappiness (anger, fear, frustration, etc.) is often a sign that I've lost sight of what I want.

... that values are the soul's guidance system to fulfillment.

... that time is indeed relative: the less I worry about it, the more I have.

... that we make time for that which is truly important to us.

... that it pays to keep my toolbox up-to-date and well maintained.

... that appreciating differences in others is enhanced if I learn from them.

... that we are like radio tuners, set to receive certain frequencies. When we raise our standards, the message comes in more clearly.

... that we are who we have learned to be.

... to challenge and scrutinize everyone who says they know, including myself.

... that the time and energy that many of us crave is hiding in cluttered corners and closets.

... that it is extremely important to thank every person who has contributed to who I am and what I believe.

... to CHILL OUT!

... to keep troubles to myself and to share joys with others.

... that to the extent that I allow questions to flow through me, their answers will come to me.

... that I have special skills and talents, requiring an investment to be fully developed.

... that the spirit guides, the heart chooses and the mind implements.

I Have Learned...

... that we cannot change yesterday, but today is here and now and we can use it well.

... that there are really no "do-overs" in life.

... that there is a child in each of us who loves to play.

... that there is more than one truth.

... that there is no such thing as a 5-minute job.

... that things are often much, much easier than I thought.

... that to get what I really want often means letting go of what I already have.

... to accept my children as the unique, spectacular gifts that they are.

... that I shouldn't compare myself to the best others can do but to the best I can do.

... that the opposite of love is not hate, but apathy.

... that there is nothing more rewarding than having a part in someone else's discovery of greater success and happiness.

... that we can only soar as high as our thoughts and beliefs allow us.

... that we spend most of our time on things we might have resolved long ago.

... to simplify. It is easier to read, decide on, create a file for, put away, maintain, update, review and be responsible for 60 items rather than 600.

I have learned that

time is

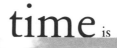

energy.

I Have Learned...

... that what people do is utterly independent of my expertise, wisdom, technical know-how, strategic brilliance or heartfelt advice.

... that we are more like our parents than we'll ever know or accept.

... to beware of saying "always" and "never."

... that whatever I project out to the Universe is what comes back to me.

... that I have all you can have, being who I am right now.

... that when we treat our jobs like they're our business, we will succeed.

... that while I screen candidates based on skill, I hire based on attitude.

... to be gentle with myself – change takes time.

... that when we lack emotional support or an outlet for our emotions, our health is almost always affected.

... to accept this moment as it is.

... that the way to get things done is to have a "Done" list, not a "To-Do" list.

... to be careful about who stays in my life.

... that we are all one; it's when we think we aren't that life gets challenging.

... that what we attract is a result of what we radiate.

... that we encounter fewer bumps if our dreams are aligned with our talents.

... to follow through.

... to be an observer of my life more often.

... that what's most important will change over time.

... to smile, make eye contact and say "thank you" to everyone who renders a service.

... that wisdom comes through lessons learned and experience, regardless of age.

... to avoid being "against" anything and to instead be "for" its opposite.

... that while opportunity favors the prepared mind, being too busy preparing prevents us from hearing the knock at opportunity's door.

... that I don't have to be ill to get better.

... that the sun shines every day and just because I can't see it, doesn't mean it's not there.

... that following my smiles uncovers my passion.

... to break monumental tasks into small pieces and frequent rewards.

... to dance and to dance like nobody's watching.

... that while our background and circumstances influence who we are, we are responsible for who we become.

... that I can't solve a problem until I admit I have one.

... that I really can keep going long after I think I can't.

... that my first thought is a big key to the solution.

I Have Learned...

... that when the student is ready the teacher really does appear.

... that what I do is NOT who I am.

... that when I feel my stomach muscles tighten it's a signal to say "no."

... that when we ask for advice we already know the answer.

... that honoring myself involves guarding my time.

... that orienting around balance and renewal helps push away the need to be busy and driven.

... to set goals without being attached to results.

... that when we truly give, we get — in the form we need it.

... that I can't use up my talents. The more they're used the more they grow.

... that tolerations, once acknowledged and written down have an almost miraculous way of getting eliminated.

... to be first or last at something new. If I'm first there's no comparison and I'll be remembered for being first. If I'm last I can learn from everyone else's mistakes.

... that learning is a life-long journey.

... to abandon the expendable.

... that the people we care most about are often the last to know it.

... that my energy is being drained by things I don't even know are happening.

I have learned that no two people
see life in exactly the same way.

I Have Learned...

... that the Universe does give us the guidance we need. Our task is to pay attention.

... that we can never laugh too much, smile too often or love too late.

... that when confidence stems from physical appearance, aging gracefully becomes more of a challenge.

... that the road less traveled is usually the one with the clearest markings and the smoothest pavement.

... that while the goal may look like a mountain, the scenery is well worth the trip.

... T.N.T: today not tomorrow.

... that venture capitalists invest in people, not just ideas.

... to listen closely to children because they speak the simple truth in simple language.

... that we can make the best use of opportunities when we stop thinking about what could go wrong.

... that unconditional love doesn't mean becoming a doormat.

... that until we heal the past, we spend our lives recreating it.

... that there's no such thing as enough hugs.

... that worry is just wasted energy.

... that friendship with my children creates an opening to an incredible life-long relationship.

... the only way to "empower" my employees is to give them power.

... to rely on my memories and to stop buying knick knacks that will be tomorrow's clutter.

... that there's probably no point in counting on winning the lottery.

... that when we trust and act on our intuition, messages come quick and clear.

... that time is a non-renewable resource; time not spent with my children this week is gone forever.

... that I cannot ever be too "sure" of anything.

... to expect most people to operate from different paradigms than my own.

... that the more we control, the less freedom we create for ourselves.

... to ask a lot of questions.

... that I am frequently my own worst enemy.

... that when we are too close to a good thing it's hard to see it.

... that keeping an idea file is like saving for the future.

... that we determine our own value. Life gives us exactly what we think we're worth.

... that we can live a blissful, joyous, life without doing drugs.

... the best cure for writer's block is a bubble bath and a glass of sherry.

... that I can have a lot of fear about something and do it anyway.

I Have Learned...

... that worry is an abuse of the imagination.

... that when all is said and done, my hardest moments pay for themselves in my personal evolution.

... that when we do what we love we are attractive.

... that we can't keep everything the same AND pursue wholesale change.

... that the people who irritate me most are those from whom I have something to learn.

... that two people holding distinctly different or even opposite points of view can both be right.

... to start with a strong question.

... to not be a scorekeeper.

... to share options rather than opinions.

... to get it out of my head and onto paper.

... to keep a running wish list in my organizer so I'm ready whenever someone asks what I'd like to receive as a present.

... that when I listen deeply and carefully, the person to whom I am listening gains strength and clarity.

... to look beyond the obvious.

... that we can choose our response.

... that truth can change instantly.

... that there are some things about us that won't ever change; acceptance is the key.

I have learned that
laughter
makes life fun .

I Have Learned...

... to keep a list of my associates' favorite things so I can buy gifts they'll appreciate.

... that there is no perfect job.

... that there is a valuable human being behind every pair of eyes.

... that there is no "right" way, but rather many possible ways.

... that with every major change, there is both gain and loss.

... that stationing myself near the door at networking events helps me meet more people.

... that I learn more from mistakes than from successes.

... that true intimacy is born out of vulnerability.

... that wealth is attracted, not chased.

... to always carry something to read.

... that grasping the hand or opportunity stretched out before me means letting go of my past.

... that our own opinions about age and experience level will hold us back far more than what others think.

... that when I am prepared to win, the door of opportunity is always wide open.

... that when we're stuck, we should ask ourselves better questions.

... that those closest to me sometimes reflect parts of my self I'd rather not see.

... that the paradigm we live in is not all that is offered to us.

... that the plans for my life will never fit into neat little boxes.

... that there are hidden gifts in baking bread and stacking wood.

... that two people can look at the exact same thing and see something totally different.

... that putting treats on my calendar makes waiting easier to endure.

... to appreciate my parents now, before they are gone.

... that my comfort zone is a danger zone.

... that twelve drummers don't make much of a band and to seek diversity in relationships.

... that when I pick my nose in the privacy of my own car, someone may be watching.

... that the world would be a better place without the words "could, should, ought and try."

... to measure success from within, not against others.

... that we are all exactly where we need to be; that life is leading each of us right were we need to go and offering us each the experiences we need.

... that too much of a good thing is terrific.

... that my role model's values and style must be compatible with my own.

... that walking on the beach is one of life's greatest pleasures.

I Have Learned...

… that we are never lost, just misguided.

… that there are few absolutes in life.

… to be suspicious of global statements, my own and those of others.

… that THINKING about something as opposed to DOING it produces radically different results.

… that the Universe will give me anything I truly want and ask for clearly.

… to always keep some cash on hand.

… that unlearning is harder than learning.

… that values are the building blocks of life purpose.

… that when I set boundaries, the people who are most worth having in my life will not only still be there, but like and respect me more.

… that the problem with doing something right the first time is that nobody appreciates how difficult it was.

… that to love your Self (and others) is to tolerate nothing.

… that what we resist most is what we need to learn.

… to make sure I am contributing more than I am costing.

… that the water feels much better once I have jumped in.

… that completing a disagreeable job today replaces 24 hours of dread and worry with 24 hours of relief and accomplishment.

… that when it comes to change, how I'm going to BE comes before what I'm going to DO.

I have learned to

follow through.

I Have Learned...

... that the world speaks to us and gives us signs along our journey; it's our job to read them.

... that when I go faster, I don't always catch-up.

... that writing is energy on paper.

... that to observe the beauty of the world without giving thought to the Artist is like accepting a gift without saying thank you.

... to look for possibilities, not limits.

... that visualization only works if it's based on strong belief.

... to make my bed every morning.

... that wealth, like freedom, is a relative term.

... that when we grow, we know.

... that there is always sunshine above the clouds.

... that getting upset with someone is usually as sign that they remind us of whatever we've not completely accepted or handled.

... to out-source or barter what I don't enjoy doing.

... that we are human beings not human doings.

... to not prejudge people or situations.

... that what I need to discover about myself I first notice in others.

... that there's an important distinction between effort and struggle.

... that we do not close sales, we open relationships.

... that there are worse places to turn for comfort than chocolate.

... that the richest people still have wants.

... that what I know is not all that I need to know.

... that we can push another person up a ladder only if they want to climb it.

... that words can be used to hurt and heal.

... that when I exercise my body, my brain comes along too.

... to double check my spell check.

... that I feel happier if I wear an orange jacket.

... that tidy people only handle things once.

... to keep an umbrella in the trunk even when I'm not expecting rain.

... that you really can talk yourself into feeling better, happier or worse.

... to always let truth lead the way. It leads whether we follow or not.

... that there's always a safe way to get what we want.

... that there's no dress rehearsal for life.

... that time together is the love language of children, friends and animals.

I Have Learned...

... that when "thank you" or "I'm sorry" is delivered with eye contact it is taken in by the soul as well as the ears.

... that to be a happy person I have to make a person happy.

... to speak clearly and use the "active" tense.

... to avoid being in the company of whiners.

... that my body can reflect what my mind is thinking.

... that watching trout jump on a glassy pond is more fun when I'm not trying to catch them.

... that I have to ask for what I want no matter how afraid I might be to do the asking.

... that we all have innate talents that are not being utilized.

... that the pain of confronting truth is an investment whose dividends are paid in peace.

... that what I say is not always what others hear and what I hear is not always what others are trying to tell me.

... that to be completely present I must be completely truthful.

... that when I set boundaries, the people who get most upset or go away were a tremendous drain on my energy anyway.

... that the path to success is not as difficult to find as it is difficult to follow.

... to put the "who" before the "what."

... to speak the truth, not jump to the solution.

I have learned to

dance and to
dance

like nobody's watching.

I Have Learned...

... that when I own my anger and do not blame my feelings on others, I retain personal strength. If I direct my anger at others I give them my power.

... to bring delight in some small, or big, way to everyone I meet.

... that we didn't choose our parents and they didn't choose us, but we can still respect and thank them for their care.

... that a baby cannot be spoiled by hugs.

... that there is someone for everyone.

... that true leaders ask, they do not assume.

... that when people criticize others, they are even harsher critics of themselves.

... to not rely on yesterday's successes to carry me into tomorrow.

... that virtually every conflict begins when someone wants to control another.

... there's an important distinction to be made between credentials and genuine competence.

... there would be far fewer people in the world if childbirth was left to male volunteers.

... to always have a contingency plan.

... that I feel a greater sense of accomplishment when I finish something ahead of the deadline.

... to question all assumptions.

... that when I don't have time to enjoy life, I should just pick out a tombstone because I've stopped living.

... that the springboard for forgiveness is a heartfelt apology.

... to exit cars curbside whenever possible.

... that I can't coach devoted "yeah, but-ers."

... the most beautiful sound in the world is the music of another human voice shattering the silence of a lonely day.

... that watching the sunrise can change my whole day.

... to seek simple solutions to complex issues.

... to let people know their gift or gesture is still appreciated by saying thank you again long after they have forgotten it.

... that work is an activity, not a place.

the end

Contributors

—Ami Olstein, amio@aloha.net

—Marian Slaman, marians@interlog.com

—Andrea Lacy, mark@lacy.vt.com

—Ann Fisher, arf@HK.Super.NET

—Barbara Hannah, bhcoach@mindspring.com

—Ann McAllister, coachamca@aol.com

—Beth Pugh, MsCoach4U@aol.com

—Christina Marshall, Christina@EduCoach.com

—Annie O'Hara, aeoglb@nwlink.com

—Arline Berman, bizcoach@ix.netcom.com

—Barb Simasko, Barb Simasko@Omegacoach.com

—Chelsea Brown Callicott, cbc@catalyst-coaching.com.

—Michele Lisenbury, director@attractionu.com

—Nancy Baker, b1nancy@aol.com

—Nancy Gerber, nbg@pla-netx.com

—Nancy Guy, nguycpa@home.com

—Nancy Partington, NPartin360@aol.com

—Nikki Sweet, NSSweet@aol.com

—Pat Miller, patmil@mindspring.com

—Pete Walsh, PeteWalsh@compuserve.com

—Peter Farmer, petefarmer@email.msn.com

—Phyllis Del Pico, ICoachUWin@pdq.net

—Rachael Lewis, Rachael@winning.com

—Rob Hershfield, rob@plan-be.com

—Robert Alderman, per4m2000@aol.com

—Sandi Stewart Epstein, SLSE123@AOL.COM

—Sandra Schrift, sschrift@grossmont.k12.ca.us

—Sandy Vilas, lasercoach@aol.com

—Sharon Day, sharonday@juno.com

—Sharon Ragsdale, smragsdale@mindspring.com

—Sheila Kutner, SheilaKut@aol.com

—Simon Reilly, coach@executivecoach.bc.ca

—Sue Seel, coachnow@aol.com

—Susan Abrams, swacoach@bcn.net

—Temple Porter, COACHME123@aol.com

—Terrence M. O'Neill, integr8@albany.net

—Megan Davis, Megandavis@aol.com

—Terry Anderson, drcoach@rogers.wave.ca

—Barbara Druker, barbarad@pacbell.net

—Bonny Henderson, hndrsn@erols.com

—Bruce St.John, BStJohn@aol.com

—Damian Nash, Damian@LoveU.com

—Cindy Uskoski, CINDY13@aol.com

—Dawn M. Osborn, M.S., dmocoach@aol.com

—Debbie Call, Coachdeb@eos.net

—Debra O'Harra, doharra@aimintl.com

—Diane Henderson, Trainassoc@aol.com

—Diane Longstreet, RDCoach@compuserve.com

Contributors

-Lenore Mewton, LMewton@aol.com

-Marjorie Wall Hofer, careerscoach@usa.net

-Kathy Pike, kathyp@tesser.com

-Meg Bentley, mpbent@cmn.net

-Kay Rose, KRoseblack@aol.com

-Mad Homan, gracecoach@aol.com

-Madeleine Homan, MHoman@StraightlineCoaching.com

-Madelyn Griffith-Haynie, mgh@addcoach.com

-Margo Chisholm, margo@tothesummit.com

-Melaney Sreenan, Ph.D., mksnan@email.msn.com

-DJ Mitsch, teamcoach@mitsch.com

-Don Edberg, don@coachu.com

-Doug Hudiburg, dhudiburg@email.msn.com

-Edie Pereira , www.erecoach.com

-Edmond E. Frank & Shawna Lovejoy,
    TAGCOACH@ix.netcom.com

-Elizabeth Carrington and Damian Nash, www.loveu.com,
    elizabeth@loveu.com

-Elizabeth Carrington, elizabeth@carringcoach.com

-Frankie Elston, Frankie.Elston@dial.pipex.com

-George Copsey, GeoNelson@aol.com

-Mary Sigmann, HarmonyPro@aol.com

-Ginger Cockerham, COACHGMC@aol.com

-Ginger Jenksi, MagellanGJ@compuserve.com

I have learned that

when we are too close to a

good thing

it's hard to see it.

Contributors

—Jerry Overton, playercoach@independence.net

—Greg Eller, coachgreg@nacs.net

—Hope Green, richergreen@worldnet.att.net

—Judy Santos, coach@judysantos.com

—Jackie Nagel, jnagel@silverlink.net

—Jenny Swanepoel, ASwanepoel@aol.com

—Jo Hawkins Donovan, karamu@execpc.com

—Joeann Fossland, Joeann@aol.com

—John Taylor, taylors@kudos.net

—Ginger Stuckemeyer, gingers@execpc.com

—Judy Godinez, Judyg110@aol.com

—Karen Copeland, KCOPE415@aol.com

—James Caldwell, james@businessplus.net

—Gail Sylvester, lifecoach@coachpartnership.co.za

—Lyn Christian, lyn_christian@7habits.com

—John Glass, jglassy@aol.com

—Bob Herpe, Coach, coachbob@bobherpe.com

—Sam Berman, Coachsam@neo.lrun.com

—Ron Mudge, ronmudge@att.net

—Thomas J. Leonard, thomas@thomasleonard.com

—Hannah S. Wilder, wiseheart@mindspring.com

—Coen de Groot, Coen@enterprise.net

—Linda R. Dominguez, lrdominguez@earthlink.net

—Jaye Myrick, Myjay@aol.com

—Nancy A. Henry, StAnnie2@aol.com

—Nanice M. Ellis, MagikStarz@aol.com

—Judi Talesnick, jtalesnick@aol.com

—Diana Robinson, Ph.D., diana@choicecoach.com

—Gerard "Jerry" Alex, REINVENT99@aol.com

—Mark Pistorius, lawcoach@onramp.net

—Marlene Elliott, marlene@marlene.net

—Jayne Garrett, focusunltd@aol.com

—Gillian, GJPCoach@aol.com

—Karen Ormiston, karen@kocoach.demon.co.uk

—Julie Leong, computrends@hevanet.com

—Jill Berquist, jillberq@aol.com

—Gretchen Little, glittle@netins.net

—Keith Collins, Incondition@msn.com

—Diana Keel, CoachDianaKeel@btinternet.com

—Leonette P. Joseph, elpeajay@worldnet.att.net

—Dr. Jim Vuocolo, jim@soulbusiness.com

—Sandra Hammar, shammar@compuserve.com

—Jeffrey T. Igoe, jigoe@mail.utexas.edu

—Timothy JohnPress, headcoach@writeme.com

—Keith Rosen, KeithRosen@ProfitBuilders.com

—Lynne Christen, lyncoach@hurricane.gnt.net

—Bill Cumming, billcummingcoach@prodigy.net

—Randa McIntosh, randa@easystreet.com

Curious About Becoming a Coach?

If the idea of becoming a coach, or learning the set of coaching skills, appeals to you, then I invite you to call 1-800-48COACH, visit http://www.coachu.com or email info@coachu.com. Coach U is in the business of training coaches (over 2,600 as of May 1999) from every state in the U.S. and 30 other countries. Coach U's Coach Training Program is recognized as the most advanced and comprehensive training of its kind.

Each month, Coach U hosts a free call-in session called Coaching Q&A, where you can find out more about coaching, what it takes to become a coach, what you learn in the Coach Training Program and how to build a practice. Several other free sessions are also available to give you a feeling for the program and to help you identify the most fitting professional development path for you.

You can also view – and register for – free coach-related classes at TeleClass.com, along with scores of other classes at the world's largest listing of TeleClasses, at http://www.teleclass.com.

COACH U